Three Television Plays

2 722152

Mrs Lawrence Will
Chariot of Fire
When the Bough

Books should be returned on or

before the date stamped above

unless a renewal has been granted.

First published in 1975 by
Davis-Poynter Limited
20 Garrick Street   London WC2E 9BJ

Copyright   ©   1975 by Tony Parker

ISBN 0 7067 0157 7

Printed in Great Britain by
Biddles Limited Guildford Surrey

CONTENTS

Mrs Lawrence Will Look After It

For Margaret Bramall

MRS LAWRENCE WILL LOOK AFTER IT was first shown on
BBC-1 in August 1968, and repeated in 1969.

Freda Wills .... MARY MILLER

Stanley Maxwell .... RAY SMITH

John Black .... BARRY JACKSON

Mrs Lawrence.......... CONSTANCE CHAPMAN

It was produced by Irene Shubik and directed by John Mackenzie.

In this play, Tony Parker is concerned with child-welfare
and the attitudes some parents adopt towards their
children. When Mrs Lawrence collapses in the street
two constables call at her home to check on her children.
To their horror they find in the house thirteen unattended
children. Gradually the picture is pieced together: the
parents found and their feelings for their children revealed.

CAST

MRS LAWRENCE
JOHN BLACK, a reporter
SISTER SWEET
NURSE PICKERING
NURSE BOON
NURSE HUTCHINSON
NURSE LONGMAN
DOCTOR DHOBI
PC ROBERTSON
PC DENT
BRUCE HAMILTON, aged $3\frac{1}{2}$
BILLY TODD, aged 4
JEAN LAWRENCE, aged $4\frac{1}{2}$
MR DARTON, newspaper proprietor
FREDA WILLS   )
) social workers
STANLEY MAXWELL)
FRED TRUELOVE, photographer
WARD SISTER
MRS WATTS
RONALD CAPE
MISS HAMILTON
COUNCILLOR PERCIVAL
JOAN PERCIVAL
MISS HEPWORTH, County Children's Officer
JANE EVANS
KATE NOLAN
VALERIE CHAPMAN
MICHAEL COLLINS
STEPHANIE WARD
MRS MILLS
MR LOW
TERRY ALLEN
LINDA ALLEN
MR BANCROFT
MRS BANCROFT
PETER UNWIN

POLICEMEN, NURSES, PORTERS, AMBULANCE DRIVER
and ATTENDANT.

A busy suburban High Street, and out doing her morning
shopping in it MRS LAWRENCE, a stout middle-aged
woman, suddenly collapses on the pavement. Close-up of
her face; her skin is pallid and damp with perspiration, her
lips are blue, her breathing is shallow and her eyes are
closed. Our view of her is constantly obscured by the bodies
and arms and hands of people gathering round to see what has
happened.

Someone lifts her head, someone else rubs one of her hands.
A shopkeeper comes out of his shop with an assistant, then
gesticulates at him to go back in the shop and 'phone for an
ambulance. A uniformed POLICEMAN appears and kneels
by her, at the same time trying to keep back the onlookers.

A little further up the street JOHN BLACK, a reporter on the
local newspaper, is just coming out of a tobacconist's, and is
about to get into his car when he notices the disturbance and
walks along the pavement to see what is happening. He is in
his late 20s, beginning to go bald, and 'sportily' but not
expensively dressed; he has not been as successful in his life
or in his career as he would have liked.

CUT TO an ambulance threading its way through the traffic
towards the scene, its light flashing and its bell ringing.

By the unconscious woman on the pavement both the
POLICEMAN and JOHN BLACK separately are unsuccessfully
questioning bystanders to try and find out what has happened
and who the woman is. BLACK touches the POLICEMAN on
the arm, pointing at the handbag from her shopping-basket
which has rolled into the gutter.

The ambulance pulls in at the edge of the pavement; the
DRIVER and ATTENDANT get out, open the doors at the
back, take out a stretcher, and ease the unconscious woman
onto it. Having found and looked at the pension-book in her
handbag, the POLICEMAN tells the AMBULANCE DRIVER
her name and address and hands the bag and her shopping-
basket to him, and they are loaded into the ambulance on the
stretcher with her. As its doors are closed and it pulls
away, the POLICEMAN reports the incident back to his

headquarters on the radio clipped to his breast-pocket; at the same time JOHN BLACK takes out a note book and jots down her name and address, which we see over his shoulder as he writes... Mrs E. Lawrence, 106 Lyndhurst Avenue.

Light flashing and bell ringing, the ambulance begins to pick up speed and we stay with it through the traffic as the title is superimposed:-

MRS LAWRENCE WILL LOOK AFTER IT

CUT TO the ambulance swinging in through a hospital's gates, turning and backing swiftly to the entrance to the Casualty Department: as it stops the ATTENDANT jumps out, opens the doors, and he and the DRIVER help a hospital PORTER transfer the stretcher to a trolley and wheel it inside. So far there has been no audible dialogue apart from half-heard phrases from the various people involved.

Within the hospital's busy Casualty Department which is in full swing dealing with a stream of admissions, the latest is dealt with swiftly and smoothly. The Department is in the charge of SISTER SWEET; she is 30, dark and good looking, but with a name that does not fit her nature since she regards all junior nurses as irresponsible and lazy. As she can do and does ten things all at the same time, quickly, calmly and efficiently, she expects the same standard from everyone else and harries them constantly so that one day they too might turn into good Casualty Sisters, though her manner suggests it would be a miracle if they ever did. Four in particular - Nurses PICKERING, BOON, HUTCHINSON and LONGMAN, all young, are on the receiving-end of her instructions and criticisms.

The Casualty Officer is DOCTOR DHOBI, a small and softly-spoken Indian, who is moving round from patient to patient as each is admitted, estimating the extent and urgency of each one's need and quietly issuing instructions to the nurses.

As the unconscious MRS LAWRENCE is wheeled into a side cubicle and moved from the trolley onto a bed in it by one of the ambulance ATTENDANTS, a PORTER and a NURSE, SISTER SWEET issues an unending stream of questions,

instructions and, where necessary, criticisms, but without
any suggestion of anxiety or panic. At the same time she
tries to get some information from MRS LAWRENCE, to test
how fit she is to understand.

SISTER SWEET: (To the AMBULANCE ATTENDANT.)
Do you know who she is? (He shakes
his head.) No relatives have been
contacted? (He shakes his head again.)
Nurse Boon, tell Doctor Dhobi the
patient who collapsed in the High
Street's here; he's down there. (To
MRS LAWRENCE.) What's your name?
Can you tell me your name? (No
answer.) Just lie still, you're going to
be all right, don't worry, we'll look
after you. (To the AMBULANCE
ATTENDANT as he goes.) Thank you
George. Nurse Pickering, don't just
stand and look at her, loosen her
clothing. Nurse Hutchinson, run after
the ambulance attendant and ask him if
they brought her handbag, her name and
address ought to be in that. I said run.
Pickering, don't push her about, if you
can't get her coat off cut the buttons.
Nurse Boon, did you tell Doctor Dhobi?
Longman, that mother in the cubicle
over there with her little girl, ask her
to leave her alone and wait in the
waiting-room, she's making her worse.
Boon, how much longer are you going to
keep that man over there waiting for his
new dressing? (To MRS LAWRENCE.)
How are you feeling? Can you tell me
how you're feeling?

MRS LAWRENCE: (Moaning) Home... got to go home...

SISTER SWEET: Nurse Boon where are you going, didn't
I tell you to tell Doctor Dhobi to - oh
it's all right he's coming, go on and get
on with that dressing I told you to.

MRS LAWRENCE:	Go... home...
DR DHOBI:	(Who has come into the cubicle and is bending over her.) Yes, yes of course, but first we must make you better musn't we? (He begins his examination of her: over his shoulder.) What is this lady's name please Sister?
SISTER SWEET:	One of the nurses has gone to try and find out, Doctor. (She is watching what he is doing and can guess at what the diagnosis is likely to be, so she begins issuing instructions to an unseen nurse to save time.) Nurse, ring Ward Seven, tell them we've a lady collapsed in the street with a suspected perf. She'll probably be going straight to theatre and then coming along to them.
DR DHOBI:	(Quietly, as he examines MRS LAWRENCE.) Is there pain here? Here? (Quietly over his shoulder.) Who is on theatre call this morning please?
SISTER SWEET:	Mr Watts, Doctor. Perforated? (He nods, and she needs no further spur.) Nurse Hutchinson, ring theatre and ask Mr Watts to come down please. Nurse Longman, fetch a Ryles tube for this patient and fix up a drip. Pickering, bring me a consent form please, come along!
HUTCHINSON:	(Rushing about.) Yes Sister.
LONGMAN:	(Rushing about.) Yes Sister.
PICKERING:	(Rushing about.) Mr Watts is on his way down, Sister.
SISTER SWEET:	(As DOCTOR DHOBI comes out of the cubicle.) There's a man waiting to be seen in Cubicle Three, Doctor Dhobi please. Nurse Boon, did you find out her name?

BOON: Mrs Lawrence, Sister.

(SISTER SWEET goes into the cubicle.
MRS LAWRENCE now has her eyes
open; but they are misted with pain.)

SISTER SWEET: (Fairly brusque.) Now then Mrs
Lawrence and how are you feeling? You
have been a silly girl haven't you, you
shouldn't have let it get to this stage
you know. Never mind, we're soon
going to get you right. Can you understand me Mrs Lawrence - we've got to
do an operation, do you understand - so
I want you to sign this form for me,
will you? Just here, come along now,
I'll help you, that's it, that's the way.

(Without ceremony SISTER SWEET puts
the pen in MRS LAWRENCE's hand and
guides it across the consent form,
almost forging the signature. When it
is done MRS LAWRENCE in a moment
of comparative lucidity suddenly grasps
SISTER SWEET's arm and manages to
force out a few words through the pain.)

MRS LAWRENCE: Home... I've got to go home.

SISTER SWEET: We'll have you home in no time, now
you just forget about everything, we'll
soon have you home.

MRS LAWRENCE: Children... at home.

SISTER SWEET: Yes we'll see to that for you, now don't
you worry, they'll be looked after.
How many children have you got Mrs
Lawrence?

(But MRS LAWRENCE has relapsed into
unconsciousness. Nurses LONGMAN
and PICKERING come into the cubicle,
pushing a trolley of equipment. SISTER
SWEET goes out.)

SISTER SWEET: Be as quick as you can. Has either of you told Mr Watts? Then where is he?

(SISTER SWEET goes down the Department to attend to another patient. On the way she stops at a 'phone on the wall and dials a single-digit number, then leans back against the wall directing the activities of the Department while she carries on the conversation.)

Casualty Sister here, get me the police please. Nurse, don't do that. Hello? This is the Casualty Sister at St George's - we've just had a woman brought in collapsed in the street with a perforated duodenal. We've got to operate on her right away. Longman, I told you to put that mother in the waiting-room; well put her back again. Hello, sorry, yes - her name's Mrs Lawrence; L-A-W-R-E-N-C-E, she lives at a hundred and six Lyndhurst Avenue. She's worried about her children she's left at home, could you attend to it please? (Signalling down the Department.) In that first cubicle Mr Watts. Hutchinson, go and tell Doctor Dhobi Mr Watts is here. (Into the 'phone.) Yes, I'd be glad if you would, thank you. One-o-six, that's right, good bye. (She hangs up the receiver and glances at her watch.) Doesn't look as though there's going to be any bloody coffee for anyone this morning.

(CUT TO the numerals 106 on the gate post of a small semi-detached council house of which the front garden has been consistently neglected. The picture is obscured by a police panda-car coming to a halt in front of it. Out of it gets a round-faced and very young

policeman, PC ROBERTSON. He opens
the gate and goes up the path. Next
door at 104 a curtain at the front window
is pulled back. PC ROBERTSON rattles
the knocker on the letter box. No reply.
He knocks on the door, tries to go round
to the back, but his way is barred by a
high fence at right angles across the side
path. We see him knock yet again at the
front door, then go to the front window,
but he cannot see inside because the
curtains are drawn. Finally he climbs
over the wall into the garden of 104.

The driver of the police car, PC DENT,
has now got out and walked up to the
gate. The woman at 104 opens her
front door. She is in the middle of
cleaning the house through, having only
just moved in; it is obvious from her
brief conversation with PC ROBERTSON
that she knows nothing about 106. PC
ROBERTSON shrugs back at PC DENT,
climbs back into the garden of 106 and
bangs the door again.

PC ROBERTSON is now about to come
down the path and consult with DENT.
The sudden loud crying of a baby from
inside 106 stops him. He pauses:
more crying is heard.)

PC ROBERTSON: (To DENT.) There's kids in there, I'll
have to break the door.

(PC DENT goes back to the police car
to report on its radio back to HQ. PC
ROBERTSON takes out his stick and
prods it sharply through the glass of the
door above the Yale lock, then gingerly
puts his hand through the hole to open
the door.

From the hallway we see ROBERTSON's hand coming in and turning the lock: he comes inside. The hallway is faintly lit from a side window. On his left doors lead to the front and back rooms: straight ahead of him is the door to the kitchen. We are positioned there: and we see him looking surprised.)

PC ROBERTSON: (Hesitantly) Erm- hello then.

(Two little boys are playing in the kitchen and have come out to go down the hall towards him. One is BRUCE HAMILTON who is $3\frac{1}{2}$, and the other is BILLY TODD who is 4. They have a toy fire engine, a carving knife and a cardboard box which they are cutting up and putting on top of an oil heater by the kitchen door. One of them is making hose-pipe and fire engine noises.)

BILLY: (Not greatly concerned.) You're a policeman.

PC ROBERTSON: That's right son, yes.

BILLY: I'm going to be a policeman.

BRUCE: I'm not, I'm going to be a fireman.

PC ROBERTSON: (Seeing BILLY hacking at the cardboard with the carving knife.) Here, you shouldn't be playing with things like that son, you might - eh, that fire's not lit is it?

BRUCE: No, the fireman put it out.

PC ROBERTSON: Come on now give that to me, there's a good lad.

(PC ROBERTSON takes the knife from BILLY. As he does so the sound of crying comes from the front room on his left. He pushes open the door, but

cannot see anything inside because the
curtains are drawn. He tries the light
switch, but the bulb has gone. He feels
his way carefully through the shadowy
furniture, of which there is a great deal,
then pulls back the curtains at the
windows to let some light in. He turns;
and stands transfixed.

The camera swings slowly round the
room, showing us what he sees.

There are six assorted babies and
toddlers in this room: one of them is on
cushions in an arm chair pushed round
against the wall so it can't fall out, one
is in a washing-basket on the floor, one
is in the pulled-out bottom drawer of an
old chest of drawers, two of them are
propped up in an old drop-side cot, and
one is on the sofa.

One is coloured. They are all drowsy,
pale, listless, irritable: several are
rather dirty with jam and crumbs on
their faces: one has an eye infection.

As PC ROBERTSON stands there dumb-
struck, another sound gradually strikes
him - that of squealing and yelling from
other children coming from the back
room. Dazed, he goes out of the front
room to the hall and turns into the back
room; again the camera shows what he
sees.

This room is not in darkness. There
are another seven children here. The
eldest is JEAN LAWRENCE, a dark-
haired pretty little girl of $4\frac{1}{2}$, who is
fighting over a toy on the floor with
another child, while the other five are
again in different unlikely places round

the room. One is in a kind of cage constructed of chairs, another is in a rickety carry-cot on a stand, and so on.

PC ROBERTSON stands, blinks, opens his mouth, shuts it again - then suddenly pulls himself together, and rushes down the hall to the front door, shouting.)

PC ROBERTSON: Alf! Eh, Alf! Come 'ere! Alf, for Christ's sake!

(CUT TO interior of hospital operating theatre. MRS LAWRENCE is on the table and the anaesthetic mask descending on her face into the camera obliterates the picture.

CUT TO a very shapely pair of female legs under a very short mini-skirt. They belong to a shorthand-typist in the office of THE GAZETTE, the local newspaper. The office is not very large, or grand, and has glass partitions. JOHN BLACK is dictating to the girl while he sits with his feet up on his desk. His collar is undone, he is smoking, and he is trying to concentrate on his dictation.)

JOHN BLACK: ... and the extreme shortage of sporting facilities for local inhabitants is now reaching scandalous lengths. The whole problem is daily rising higher and higher on the list of things we want to look at, and when the true situation is fully revealed - (The 'phone rings: he flips up the receiver.) Black. No, he's not here at the moment, Mr Darton. No, Morgan's out as well. Yes OK Sir. (Replaces receiver.) Have to leave that for a bit love, the boss is coming in.

(Unaware of and unconcerned about the
effect she has on him, the girl gets up
and goes out, yawning: after all, she's
17, she has her own boy friend of 18,
and to her JOHN BLACK is just another
middle-aged man. JOHN BLACK wishes
he was younger and lights another
cigarette.

MR DARTON, the proprietor and
managing editor comes in; he is elderly,
grey-suited, and a big fish in a small
pool.)

MR DARTON: What are you supposed to be doing
               Black?

JOHN BLACK: (Taking his feet off his desk.) An
               attacking piece for the sports page Sir,
               I thought it was about time someone
               wrote about the lack of -

MR DARTON: What time will Wheaton be back?

JOHN BLACK: He's gone to the chemical works,
               there's been some kind of accident
               there with a -

MR DARTON: And Morgan's out too? Damn nuisance.
               I'm due to see the Chairman of the
               Council at half past two.

JOHN BLACK: Something important? I mean, should
               I -

MR DARTON: You're supposed to be the sports writer.

JOHN BLACK: (As sarcastically as he dare.) I have
               been known to write an odd line now and
               again about -

MR DARTON: Well I suppose there's no choice.
               Anyway, Wheaton can take it over from
               you when he gets back. There's some-
               thing going on up on the Council Estate,
               we've just had an anonymous 'phone
               call. Police breaking into a house,

MR DARTON: (Cont)	sending radio messages, flapping about. Lyndhurst Avenue.
JOHN BLACK:	One-o-six.
MR DARTON:	Yes that's right. You know something about it?
JOHN BLACK:	A woman collapsed in the High Street this morning, I wrote her name down. (From his notebook.) Yes, Mrs Lawrence, one-o-six.
MR DARTON:	I don't know whether it's anything or not. Anyway, go up and find out. (Opens office door.) And before lunch if you don't mind.
	(MR DARTON goes out. JOHN BLACK doesn't like the implied reproof, particularly as it's justified. He grimaces, gathers up his note book, sticks it and a pen into a pocket of his jacket hanging on a peg; then as he is about to go out an idea strikes him. He picks up the 'phone and makes an internal office call.)
JOHN BLACK:	Ted? Look, got to go up to the Council Estate, something might be going on up there - want to come and take a few pictures? (Pause) OK, I'll buy you a beer. Yes all right, two beers. See you in a minute round the back in the car.
	(The unattended police car stands outside 106 Lyndhurst Avenue. One or two neighbours are hanging about, trying to see what is going on. The police car radio is crackling.)
POLICE RADIO:	Fox-trot Two. Come in please Fox-trot Two. Over. (Pause) Fox-trot Two report please, where are you, over.

POLICE RADIO: (Cont)	(Pause) Can you hear me Fox-trot Two, come in please, over.
	(PC DENT has come out of the front door to talk to some of the neighbours. Hearing the radio he goes down the path, leans into the car and unhooks the microphone.)
PC DENT:	Fox-trot Two to HQ. I hear you, over.
	(CUT TO interior of the house. PC ROBERTSON is trying to deal with several problems at once - to soothe one of the babies who is bawling in his arms, to keep an eye on JEAN LAWRENCE who is dragging a chair across the kitchen, and to see what BILLY and BRUCE are up to. JEAN LAWRENCE drags the chair to beside the gas-stove, on which two saucepans are simmering, and starts to climb up on it.)
PC ROBERTSON:	Heh, get down you silly girl, what are you doing?
JEAN:	(Indicating tin on shelf.) Want a biscuit.
PC ROBERTSON:	Oh wait a minute can't you, I'll reach it for you, get down.
	(Carrying the baby, PC ROBERTSON edges round in the confined space of the kitchen, stumbling over children and toys and swearing under his breath. He takes down the tin.)
JEAN:	(Taking a biscuit, laconically.) He wants his nappy changed.
PC ROBERTSON:	No he doesn't he's quite all - yes well perhaps you're right. Anyhow, he'll have to wait. (He turns towards the kitchen doorway as PC DENT comes

PC ROBERTSON: (Cont)	back.) Here Alf, you're a married man, you can deal with this, he wants his -
PC DENT:	Sorry mate, you're on your own. There's been a wages job down at South-side, I've got to get over there.
PC ROBERTSON:	Hell Alf, look wait a minute, what am I -
PC DENT:	Good luck Robbie, I've got to deal with the crime wave. I've asked them to contact the Children's Department and send someone down here, it's their pigeon. See you, dadyo.
PC ROBERTSON:	Alf, for Christ's sake how am I supposed to -
	(It is too late. PC DENT has gone. JEAN LAWRENCE examines PC ROBERTSON cooly. Under her stare he shifts uneasily and does his best to smile.)
	Well, well then, and what's your name then, eh?
JEAN:	Jean Lawrence. What's yours?
PC ROBERTSON:	Erm - Arthur. (Pause) Erm, Arthur Robertson -
JEAN:	(Blandly) My uncle says all policemen are custards.
PC ROBERTSON:	(Reacting slowly.) Oh yes? Oh - does he now? I see, well how many other little - how many other children are there here like you then?
JEAN:	I dunno. I can't count.
PC ROBERTSON:	(A sudden thought strikes him and he points upwards.) There aren't any more upstairs? (JEAN shakes her head: PC ROBERTSON lets out his breath in relief.) Well what shall we do first while we're waiting?

JEAN:	(Implaccably) He wants his nappy changed.
PC ROBERTSON:	Yes, yes, well I'll - er -
JEAN:	I can do it.
PC ROBERTSON:	You can? Are you sure?
JEAN:	(Taking the baby from him, confidently.) 'Course! Anyone can do that. (She looks at him disdainfully and takes the baby out.)

(There is a sudden uproar in the front room, with several children all yelling at once. PC ROBERTSON takes a deep breath, pulls down his jacket, and makes for the door.) |
| PC ROBERTSON: | Oh Christ, oh bloody kids.

(A frosted glass office door with the words 'Child Care Officers' lettered on it. Opening it and going in is FREDA WILLS, a Senior Child Care Officer. She is 28, slim, good looking but not glamourously so; a cool, efficient and highly trained woman, fashionably dressed. At a desk in the office, talking on the telephone, is STANLEY MAXWELL. He is another Child Care Officer, junior to Freda, 36, bald, plump, and pipe-smoking. They have a good working relationship: if anyone told her she was a little in love with him she would deny it with a laugh. All the same, if she had met him ten years ago before he married and had a family...) |
| STANLEY: | (On telephone.) Yes yes, go on, go on, it's nothing. (FREDA tries to speak, but STANLEY frantically waves at her to keep quiet.) What? No! I don't believe you! Good God man, you're a |

STANLEY: (Cont)	bloody marvel! I do, I love you! (He puts the receiver down.)
FREDA:	Stanley, could you possibly have a look at this and tell me -
STANLEY:	He's got them, he's got them! He's done it!
FREDA:	You don't mean Roger's got the grants for the unmarried mothers' flats?
STANLEY:	What? Unmarried - what on earth are you - oh that, good God no, it's far more important than that. That was Jim, he's got two tickets for the Cup Final!
FREDA:	Stanley, really, won't you ever grow up?
STANLEY:	My dear girl, you couldn't possibly understand, could you? The Cup <u>Final</u>. Who cares about unmarried mothers when they've got a ticket for the Cup Final?
FREDA:	Well you should. Another of your cases has taken a slightly wrong turning. You'd better read through that. (Hands him a file.) Got a cigarette? (He indicates a packet on the desk and she helps herself.) I wonder how it is a higher proportion of your cases become pregnant than anyone else's in this office, Stanley?
STANLEY:	Miss Wills, I shall ignore that remark. (His telephone rings. He answers it while looking through the file that FREDA has given him.) Maxwell. Yes, she's here. (He passes her the telephone puffing on his pipe while he looks at the file again and tries to concentrate on it; but he is still thinking about the Cup Final.)
FREDA:	(On the telephone.) Yes, I'm the Senior Child Care Officer responsible for that area. Just a minute - what's the address

FREDA: (Cont)	again? (Making a note.) Yes, we'll attend to it. (Pause) I beg your pardon? How many? (Softly) Christ! (She puts the 'phone down.)
STANLEY:	(Looking at the file.) Miss Wills, your language is not suitable to your position.
FREDA:	All right, Stanley. There's a nice little job come up for us.
STANLEY:	(Still reading the file.) Good. (He looks up. She is no longer near his desk but is half way out through the door.) Heh wait a minute, I haven't had my lunch, what's all the -
FREDA:	You'll be lucky if you get any lunch today dear! Or tomorrow. Bring the car round the front. Tell you about it on the way.
	(In the theatre the surgeon is operating on MRS LAWRENCE. Near her head the anaesthetic-machine bag is filling and emptying.
	JOHN BLACK is driving his old sports car through the streets towards the Council Estate. Accompanying him is a fat photographer, TED TRUELOVE. He is nearing the end of his career: on this suburban newspaper he takes all his pictures wearily and unfeelingly. The car turns into a road marked 'Lyndhurst Avenue'.
	STANLEY MAXWELL and FREDA WILLS set off from outside the Children's Department Office in a Morris 1100, with STANLEY driving.
	The end of the operation on MRS LAWRENCE. She is being wheeled out of the theatre on a trolley.

The kitchen at Lyndhurst Avenue.
JOHN BLACK is talking to PC
ROBERTSON. TED TRUELOVE is
vaguely wandering about trying to get a
few pictures, without really knowing why
he is there. None of the children are
very co-operative.)

JOHN BLACK: And you mean nobody knew about it?

PC ROBERTSON: If they did, they weren't saying. Sort of
local unofficial nursery I suppose,
dump your child here and have it looked
after while you -

JOHN BLACK: And what a dump! Phew! The stink!
Wonder what was in it for the woman
who -

PC ROBERTSON: You must be joking, mate. Two or
three quid a week each, she can't miss.

JOHN BLACK: My God, people like that ought to be
shot. (To a child.) Hello son, what's
your name then?

(BILLY TODD is passing. JOHN
BLACK does a full knees bend to get
down to his level, catches hold of him
and faces TED TRUELOVE while he
talks to the child.)

Try and get this, Ted. (To the child.)
Where's your tongue gone then, eh?
What's your name, don't you know your
name? Go on, tell me your name, tell
me your name and I'll see if I can't get
it printed in a newspaper for you, eh?

(JOHN BLACK suddenly becomes aware
that someone else has come in: perhaps
because of the expression on PC
ROBERTSON's face. He looks up and
sees FREDA WILLS in the doorway,
with STANLEY MAXWELL behind her.

JOHN BLACK nods cheerfully and
stands.)

JOHN BLACK: 'Morning!

FREDA: (Coldly to PC ROBERTSON.) My name is Miss Wills, I'm from the Children's Department. Who are these men?

JOHN BLACK: Black's my name, John Black, and this is Ted Truelove. How do you do? Well this is a mess all right, isn't it?

FREDA: (Ignores him: to PC ROBERTSON.) How did they get in?

JOHN BLACK: We're from the Press.

FREDA: Obviously. I'd be glad if you'd leave, please.

JOHN BLACK: Here now wait a minute, we're only doing our job, we've as much right to be here as -

(TED TRUELOVE lifts his camera to try and take a picture of JOHN BLACK and FREDA WILLS arguing. MAXWELL stands in front of him and smiles pleasantly.)

STANLEY: You click that shutter and I'll boot the camera out of one window and you out of another.

JOHN BLACK: (To PC ROBERTSON.) Are you going to stand there and let them threaten us?

PC ROBERTSON: (Embarrassed, knowing he shouldn't have let them in.) I think it'd be better if you did as the young lady asked.

JOHN BLACK: (To FREDA.) Look, I'm on your side. People should know about this, that it goes on. Here's a woman making a fortune out of -

FREDA: My concern at the moment is with the

FREDA: (Cont)	children. I haven't time for a discussion about ethics, thank you.
JOHN BLACK:	Look, I've got a job to do and I'm bloody well -
FREDA:	So have I. I am a Senior Child Care Officer, this house is now my responsibility, and I'm asking you to leave it. If necessary I shall request this Police Officer to eject you. (JOHN BLACK looks at PC ROBERTSON; but he's going to get no help from him. He looks at TED TRUELOVE, who is totally disinterested. And he looks at STANLEY MAXWELL who is puffing amiably on his pipe.)
JOHN BLACK:	Oh, I see, County Hall covering-up eh? All right Ted, come on, we've got some work to do. (He nods at FREDA and STANLEY.) I wouldn't miss Friday's 'Gazette' if I were you.
FREDA:	(Calmly) See them off the premises will you Stanley, and then have a quick look round the house please will you? (JOHN BLACK and TED TRUELOVE go out, followed by STANLEY MAXWELL. PC ROBERTSON stands on one foot and then on the other.)
PC ROBERTSON:	I'm very sorry, Miss, I wasn't really thinking, I was a bit taken up with - my driver was going to help me out but he's got a call to -
FREDA:	(Unbending a little.) Well never mind, but how did they get on to it so quickly?
PC ROBERTSON:	Neighbours, I suppose. Some people'll 'phone a newspaper before they'd call the fire brigade.

FREDA:	What's the position, can you tell me?
PC ROBERTSON:	At least thirteen children here, Miss. None of them hers as far as I could tell.
FREDA:	(Quietly) Yes I see ... That reporter getting in puts rather a different complexion on it.
PC ROBERTSON:	I haven't found out yet who any of them belong to. But Headquarters sent a message to say they were trying to contact the woman's daughter, she works at the Co-op over the other side of the town.
FREDA:	How far's High Acres from here?
PC ROBERTSON:	About half a mile, Miss, top of the hill.
FREDA:	One of our peripatetic house mothers lives there, Mrs Watts, number seventeen. Could you go up and ask her if she'd come here as soon as possible?
PC ROBERTSON:	Yes certainly, Miss, number seventeen. I'll go right away - what did you say she was again, Miss?
FREDA:	A peripa - you know, a sort of casual house mother we use in different places as required. (PC ROBERTSON nods.) Her name is Mrs Watts. Thank you for all you've done. (She smiles.)
	(PC ROBERTSON goes out just as STANLEY comes back in from the hallway.)
STANLEY:	Thirteen, plus one mangy cat. House a bit untidy but I've seen worse, some of the kids not as clean as they might be, one or two under-fed. One definitely under-nourished, and one with an eye infection that needs attention right away. Six oil stoves, none of them lit, toilet doesn't flush, stale biscuits under the

STANLEY: (Cont)	furniture, three dead tadpoles in a jar. We'll have her for cruelty to animals, anyway.
FREDA:	She's a daughter at work who's been sent for. (She is at the stove, looking in the pans.)
STANLEY:	Another daughter? There's one here, the little girl with long black hair, her name's Jean Lawrence. (Looking round.) What about the Health Visitor, for God's sake - she must have known what was going on here.
FREDA:	This is Mrs Green's area, isn't it? She's been in hospital a couple of months. There've been two or three different ones filling in since. Boiled potatoes and mince, a bit over-done perhaps, but - well Stanley, thirteen plates please.
STANLEY:	Do you mind? I haven't had my lunch - fourteen.
FREDA:	(Smiles, takes off her jacket, rolls up the sleeves of her blouse, finds and puts on an apron.) Doesn't smell too bad actually - better make it fifteen. (MRS LAWRENCE is just coming round from the anaesthetic in a curtained-off bed in a hospital ward. Her eyes flutter, they open, and she tries to recollect what has happened. She tries to lift her head, and groans. A NURSE is sitting at the bedside waiting for her to regain consciousness.)
NURSE:	(Wiping MRS LAWRENCE's forehead.) Feeling a bit better now? Lie still, you're all right. (She puts her head out of the curtains round the bed.) Sister! She's coming round Sister.

(The WARD SISTER, a soft-voiced
Welsh woman, appears through the
curtains.)

WARD SISTER: Well Mrs Lawrence, you gave us a real
old fright then, didn't you? Never
mind, we got you in time. Can you lift
your head up just a little, there. (She
takes a water mug from the bedside
locker top.) Only a little sip now, not
too much.

MRS LAWRENCE: Where...

WARD SISTER: You're in hospital, you've had an
operation. Collapsed in the street didn't
you now, do you remember?

MRS LAWRENCE: (Closing her eyes.) What... time...
is...

WARD SISTER: It was this morning, now you lie there
and rest, you're going to be all right.

MRS LAWRENCE: (Opening her eyes suddenly.) The
children - got to give them their dinner
- got to go home and -

WARD SISTER: (Smiles) Oh that's all being looked
after, there's nothing for you to worry
yourself about at all. Everything's
being taken care of for you.

(CUT TO chaos and uproar at Lyndhurst
Avenue as FREDA and STANLEY are
washing up in the kitchen and trying to
cope with the children, some of whom
are crying and others whooping around.
Despite this FREDA and STANLEY
seem to be enjoying themselves.)

FREDA: Stanley you'd better leave this drying up
to me and go and play with that child and
keep him quiet.

STANLEY: His idea of playing is whacking me over
the head with a newspaper and saying
he's a policeman.

FREDA: (Sweetly) Then you must try and direct his energies into constructive channels, musn't you?

STANLEY: Yes I read that book too - but if you'd go three children of your own like I have you'd know it wasn't quite as -

FREDA: (Gives him a joking flip with the tea towel.) Go on, grandad.

(But before STANLEY can go into the other room there is a knock at the front door; he goes instead down the hall to open it and admit MRS WATTS who is a small elderly and energetic north-country woman. Hardly is she inside the door when she has taken off her coat and hung it up, found an apron and put it on, and rolled up her sleeves.)

MRS WATTS: 'Ello Mr Maxwell I came as soon as I could, sorry I'm late but I 'ad to finish off me washing, afternoon Miss Wills, well this is a right old 'ow d'yer do isn't it, I've brought me things in case you wanted me to stop over tonight.

FREDA: Hello Mrs Watts, thank you for coming. Well everything's more or less under control (STANLEY grimaces.) so I'll leave it to you and Mr Maxwell. I'll have to make a few 'phone calls, ask the hospital if the woman's well enough to be seen yet, and I suppose I'd better report to Miss Hepworth too, Stanley.

STANLEY: Don't you think she might feel bound to come and give us the benefit of her supervision if you did?

FREDA: That's a risk we'll have to run.

MRS WATTS: (Mimicking MISS HEPWORTH.) 'Dear me, and what 'ave we here? Sew kind of you Mrs Watts to give us a hend'. Ah

MRS WATTS: (Cont)	well, that's what you get from the gaffer. 'Ow many is there 'ere then?
STANLEY:	Thirteen.
MRS WATTS:	Go on, you're kiddin'! Thirteen! Oh well - all right then, the sooner we get started the better eh? (She goes out into the other room to see the children. FREDA puts on her jacket, goes down the hall, glances briefly at herself in the mirror, and goes out.) (CUT TO FREDA talking to the WARD SISTER.)
WARD SISTER:	...well I didn't know all that. I must say I can put up with most things, but neglecting children really makes my blood boil. We'll get her better, and then I hope you send her to prison where she belongs.
FREDA:	I think it's a bit too soon to start jumping to conclusions. At the moment my main concern is the children, and finding out who they belong to. I won't stop with her very long.
WARD SISTER:	She's in the end bed at the bottom round the corner. The anaesthetic's not worn off yet, I don't think you'll get a lot of sense out of her. She's already got a visitor with her, by the way. (FREDA has not heard this last remark as she has started off down the ward. When she turns the corner and sees MRS LAWRENCE in bed, she also sees who is sitting there; JOHN BLACK, talking amiably to her.)
FREDA:	Mrs Lawrence? Good afternoon, I'm from the Children's Department.

JOHN BLACK: (Standing) A Senior Child Care Officer, in fact. Well I'll be getting along Mrs Lawrence. Take care of yourself; and if I were you I shouldn't talk too much to officials from County Hall. Cheerio Miss Whatsit. (He goes off down the ward.)

FREDA: Do you know that man?

MRS LAWRENCE: No, he's nice though; look, he brought me some flowers.

FREDA: He's a newspaper reporter.

MRS LAWRENCE: Yes he said his newspaper'd try and help me. Who did you say you were, love?

FREDA: I'm a Child Care Officer. May I sit down? (She doesn't wait for an answer.) And how are you feeling, Mrs Lawrence?

MRS LAWRENCE: Sore. Have these pains you know, and never done nothin'. You don't think, do you? Oh dear, but I do feel dreadful, are the children all all right, it's terrible isn't it, I'd only just slipped out for five minutes -

FREDA: Yes, they're being looked after. You must be very tired so I won't stay long. My main object at this stage is to try and help the children, not to get you into trouble, so I hope we can -

MRS LAWRENCE: Get me into trouble? Why? Looking after a few children's not -

FREDA: Not a few, Mrs Lawrence, thirteen.

MRS LAWRENCE: Yes it is a lot, I suppose, isn't it? You don't notice though do you, first one comes and then another and -

FREDA: It's far more than the regulations allow.

MRS LAWRENCE: Regulations? (She is a very simple

MRS LAWRENCE: (Cont)	woman, and she is not being devious.) But it was only for friends like, or people I knew, just to help them while they -
FREDA:	Well, we'll talk about that some other time. But you are aware, aren't you, that at least three of them are in need of medical attention?
MRS LAWRENCE:	(Pleased) That's exactly what I said. It's not right is it, neglecting them? If there's one thing I can't stand, it's neglecting children, I think their mothers ought to be prosecuted, sometimes I really do. Poor little Chrissie, and her eyes like that. Oh it's nothing, they said, we've put some ointment on them, she'll be all right in a week or two. I can tell you Miss, I was going to take her to the doctor myself tomorrow, only now this -
FREDA:	Well, I called the Doctor in, Mrs Lawrence -
MRS LAWRENCE:	Oh good! And Billy's got a nasty toe nail too, he ought to have that seen to as well, so perhaps you'd ask him -
FREDA:	But what I've got to do first is find out who they are and try and contact their parents. (Takes out a notebook.) Could you briefly give me details of them?
MRS LAWRENCE:	(Helpfully) Well, there's my Jean, she lives there doesn't she, and then there's our Betty's Eileen, sometimes she stops and sometimes she doesn't, depends how she's getting on with Jack. Had a terrible time with him you know, I've said to her over and over 'If 'e wants to marry you' I've said 'Well then 'e should marry you'. I mean it's not right is it Miss, after all if a man's -

FREDA: (Patiently) Just a moment. Two are related to you, Mrs Lawrence, is that right? Your own daughter Jean, and then you say one is your grand-daughter? Well what about the other eleven, where do they come from?

MRS LAWRENCE: (Helpfully again.) Well there's two just stops for the day, that's Bruce and Billy - no, it's three, because there's Ronnie isn't there, that's right, yes.

FREDA: Which would make eight stopping with you permanently?

MRS LAWRENCE: All the time you mean? Yes. Well no, not really, because you see Robert's with me five days a week, and then there's Teresa, well with her it's just off and on like, sometimes she does and sometimes she doesn't. And with Lillian and Laureen you see it's the same, you know what I mean, you just never know. 'Course they have a very hard time don't they those girls, it's not easy for 'em.

FREDA: (Trying to follow.) Mrs Lawrence, we've got to find out who the children's parents are and see if they can take them back, or they'll all have to go into care.

MRS LAWRENCE: Into a home you mean? Oh no, you wouldn't want to do that, they wouldn't like it. (Suddenly) I never got them their ice-cream, that was what I'd gone out for, oh isn't it a shame!

FREDA: I know you must be feeling very weak still, and I don't want to tire you, Mrs Lawrence, but I really must -

MRS LAWRENCE: 'Course you must love. Well now, I'll have to think, won't I? I'll think, and you write it down in your little book, how's that? If I picture them in my mind

MRS LAWRENCE: (Cont)	that helps. Well first of all there's little Billy Todd, he's the one with the fair hair and the lovely little round face. Now 'is mother usually comes about four. Oh and that reminds me, it's usually not long after four Mr Cape comes with his boy. Or is it this week he collects him at four and - no, that's right this week 'e brings 'im...
	(CUT TO RONALD CAPE, a small dapper man of about 40, wearing a 'bus conductor's' uniform; he is just putting a small boy in the side-car of his motor bike.
	STANLEY is sitting at the table in the kitchen at Lyndhurst Avenue. Opposite to him is MISS HAMILTON, a tall and thin-faced Scots woman in her late thirties. She is extremely embarrassed and ill-at-ease.)
STANLEY:	So if I may have your name and address?
MISS HAMILTON:	Hamilton. Edna Hamilton. Mrs Edna Hamilton. (Unhappily) Miss Edna Hamilton.
STANLEY:	(Not reacting.) And you've really never seen inside this house before today?
MISS HAMILTON:	Indeed I have not. Mrs Lawrence seemed very nice and she was recommended: you don't like to ask if you can see inside a house when people -
STANLEY:	So you've been leaving your little boy every morning for the past two weeks and -
MISS HAMILTON:	Picking him up on my way home from school, yes.
STANLEY:	How much were you paying?

MISS HAMILTON:	Thirty shillings a week: that seemed very reasonable.
STANLEY:	And your address is?
MISS HAMILTON:	(After a pause.) Thirty-one Park Road.
STANLEY:	You're a teacher?
MISS HAMILTON:	I teach at the County Primary School. Will they - must they, is it necessary for them to -
STANLEY:	No of course not, this is entirely confidential.
MISS HAMILTON:	There's not everyone you see... I was told that was why Mrs Lawrence was so sympathetic, they say her own daughter was similarly placed. Dear me I don't know what I'm going to do now.
STANLEY:	We'll try and find a place in one of the Local Authority day nurseries.
MISS HAMILTON:	Oh I wouldn't like that, they're only for - I mean they're not really very nice people who put their children in those day nurseries if you know what I mean.
STANLEY:	(Calmly) No I'm afraid I don't.
MISS HAMILTON:	I suppose men are all the same, you think it's awful, we -
STANLEY:	I don't think you're facing up to the facts, Miss Hamilton, that's all.
MISS HAMILTON:	You don't know what the facts are.
STANLEY:	No, true. What about the father?
MISS HAMILTON:	He's up in Scotland, I've no wish to -
STANLEY:	Does he pay maintenance?
MISS HAMILTON:	No he does not! And I wouldn't stoop to asking him for -
STANLEY:	You don't exactly make things easy for yourself do you?

MISS HAMILTON:	I'm not asking for sympathy thank you.
STANLEY:	I'm not offering it, I'm trying to find a way of giving practical help. What about your family?
MISS HAMILTON:	We are not in communication.
STANLEY:	(Sighs) Miss Hamilton, I think if you could come up and talk this over at the Children's Department -

(BRUCE HAMILTON, with his coat and hat on, comes in.)

BRUCE:	Mummy, that boy won't give me back my fire engine.
MISS HAMILTON:	Well never mind dear you can get it tomorrow... (And then she looks helplessly at STANLEY.)
STANLEY:	Would you come to the Department one day next week?
MISS HAMILTON:	(Dispirited) Yes, I suppose I shall have to, shan't I? (To BRUCE.) Well come along then now dear, say good afternoon to this gentleman.
BRUCE:	Bye-bye.
STANLEY:	Bye-bye Bruce.

(STANLEY takes MISS HAMILTON and BRUCE down the hall and shows them out of the front door. By the time he returns to the kitchen BETTY LAWRENCE is there, having come in through the back door. She is dark, 23, hard, plain: and a nice girl.)

BETTY:	'Oo the hell are you then, what are you doin' -
STANLEY:	I'm from the Children's Department. Are you Mrs Lawrence's daughter?

BETTY:	The Children's - do you mean the Welfare? They sent for me, Mum's 'ad to go to hospital. What's the matter, what's happened to -
STANLEY:	She's all right, as far as I know the operation's been a success: a duodenal ulcer, it burst while she was out shopping.
BETTY:	Oh my God! I told 'er, 'You ought to go to the doctor's' I said, but she wouldn't. And now this. Is it serious?
STANLEY:	I think it could be, yes. There are strict regulations about looking after children for other people -
BETTY:	What? No, I mean Mum.
STANLEY:	No, I don't think there are any complications, she'll be -
BETTY:	And what about the kids - what about them, are they -
STANLEY:	We've got some help.
BETTY:	But you'll need more. Look, after I've been up the 'ospital and seen Mum, I'll come back 'ere and give you a hand.
STANLEY:	That'd certainly be a great help. And any information you could give us about who the children belong to -
BETTY:	Yes, yes I will. God, it's ridiculous isn't it? She's not quite... I think it was since Dad died last year, been a bit funny, know what I mean? Like - like trying to give herself something to do, stop herself thinking.
STANLEY:	And making an income?
BETTY:	(A short sour laugh.) You can say that again. I said 'You don't want to let 'em get away with it Mum, they can afford it better than you can'. But oh no. 'I'm

BETTY: (Cont)	sorry Mrs Lawrence, I'm real 'ard up'. 'Oh that's all right love, just whenever you can manage it'. Go without 'er own dinner so long as the kids got enough. 'I don't feel like eating today anyway, it's me tummy playin' me up again'. I think she was frightened she'd got the same as me Dad. Well, that's it now isn't it? She'll get into trouble, will she?
STANLEY:	I honestly don't know yet. Oh and by the way, I'm afraid the local paper's got hold of it. (BETTY LAWRENCE shakes her head, worried and unable to think of anything to say.) (JOHN BLACK is beginning what he would dignify with the name of his 'research'. He's gossiping with neighbours, talking to people in the pub, going into the office of the local Registrar of Births, Deaths and Marriages. He turns through the pages, and makes notes.) (COUNCILLOR PERCIVAL, a well-built and well dressed man in his early fifties, in his large and well appointed house is answering the telephone as his daughter JOAN is going up the stairs.)
PERCIVAL:	(On the 'phone.) Yes, this is Councillor Percival speaking. The Gazette? (Pause) Look, what exactly do you want, I'm afraid I don't know what you're - (Long pause: curtly.) You must have got the wrong person, I've nothing further to say to you. (He puts down the 'phone and goes back into his study. Halfway up the stairs JOAN, a university student of 20 wearing

jeans and a floppy pullover, turns and comes down and follows him into the room.)

JOAN: (Casually) Who was that? What was it about?

PERCIVAL: Nothing, dear. Just something to do with Council business. (He studiedly starts writing.)

JOAN: (Quietly) Tell me who it was.

PERCIVAL: (Angrily) Joan, what's the matter with you, I've told you it was a mistake, it was just someone - (He realises his reaction has been revealing.)

JOAN: Why did The Gazette want you?

PERCIVAL: (Still flustered.) I've really no idea, it was about some woman... (He stops.)

JOAN: Well, go on.

PERCIVAL: (Over-calmly.) Look, I'm afraid I've got an awful lot to do -

JOAN: You said it was about some woman. (She stands and looks at him; he is unable to look directly back at her.) The Gazette? (She starts to move towards the door.) I'm sure they'd tell me what -

PERCIVAL: Joan! I forbid you to -

JOAN: (Turning) You forbid me to what? (Pause: like an arrow.) To find out what's happened to my own child? (It found its target.) Isn't that what it was about? Well? (Pause)

PERCIVAL: Look it's all over and done with Joan, we agreed that, it was what you wanted, we agreed it would be for the best -

JOAN: I wasn't even consulted! Daddy knows what's best! We'll have it adopted and

JOAN:
(Cont)
  then we can all forget all about it. Well I'm afraid it won't do. I want to know exactly -

PERCIVAL:
  Joan, you're not being fair, after all I've -

JOAN:
  Oh yes, the Chairman of the Education Committee, the Mayor-elect - his daughter couldn't have an illegitimate baby could she? (Fiercely) After all you've done! I want to know - and if you're not going to tell me -

(Silently, they confront each other.)

(The door bell rings at 106. STANLEY MAXWELL opens it and RONALD CAPE in his 'bus conductor's' uniform is there.)

RONALD CAPE:
  Good afternoon, my name's Cape, I've called to collect my boy. Mrs Lawrence in?

STANLEY:
  I'm afraid she's had to go into hospital -

RONALD CAPE:
  Oh, sorry to hear that, where's my young Ronald then?

STANLEY:
  (Vaguely waving his arm towards the front room.) Perhaps you'd like to come in and -

(RONALD CAPE needs no further invitation. He walks in, nods at MRS WATTS, picks up one of the children, and walks out with him.)

RONALD CAPE:
  Quite a full house today then? Better not bring him for a few days if she's not well, eh? Give her my regards, won't you? Cheerio.

STANLEY:
  Just a moment, could you give me your name and address, please?

RONALD CAPE:	I could - but I'd want to know why, wouldn't I?
STANLEY:	I'm a Child Care Officer, and these children are our responsibility.
RONALD CAPE:	Good luck to you then mate. But this one isn't. He's mine.
STANLEY:	I'm sorry but I have to ask you some questions. You pay Mrs Lawrence?
RONALD CAPE:	Yes, two quid a week - and well worth it. I've no complaints, can't look after 'im myself, since my wife's... You'll get no help from me if you're trying to get her into trouble, if it hadn't been for her he'd have to have gone into a home or something.
STANLEY:	Where's his mother?
RONALD CAPE:	Good question. Good afternoon. (And without another word, RONALD CAPE goes.)

(JOHN BLACK is in his car, pulling-up at the kerb outside a neat suburban semi-detached house. He gets out and, whistling, goes up the path. He rings the bell.) |
| JOHN BLACK: | Mrs Mills? Good afternoon. I'm from The Gazette - could I have a few words with you?

(The face of MISS HEPWORTH, the County Children's Officer. An elderly, grey-haired and rather forbidding woman, she is in the kitchen at Lyndhurst Avenue talking quietly to FREDA and STANLEY. She is not quite as hard as her appearance and manner suggest.) |
| MISS HEPWORTH: | So at least Freda you managed to get most of the names and addresses. |

FREDA: She was only just recovering from the
                 anaesthetic; and I imagine her memory's
                 rather vague at the best of times.

MISS HEPWORTH: But doubtless she's more careful about
                 the money.

FREDA: To be honest I'm not so sure about that.

MISS HEPWORTH: Well, what do you think we should do -
                 immediately, I mean?

FREDA: Mrs Watts is prepared to sleep here
                 tonight, and I will too.

STANLEY: And Betty Lawrence said she'd come
                 back and help.

MISS HEPWORTH: The woman's daughter? I suppose that
                 will do temporarily, but -

FREDA: I'd like to see how many of the parents
                 we could contact in twenty-four hours.

MISS HEPWORTH: It will mean a great deal of hard work
                 for you both tomorrow. Could I have a
                 look at your list, Freda? (She takes
                 FREDA's notebook when it is handed to
                 her.) I'll stay and assist Mrs Watts for
                 a while, but I can't stay too long, I have
                 to go up to the West End for a committee
                 meeting.

FREDA: One of the mothers works in Soho, Miss
                 Hepworth, would you like to call in and
                 see her?

MISS HEPWORTH: By all means - which one is it?

                 (FREDA points at a name on the list.)

FREDA: Her name's Stephanie Ward, she works
                 at a place whose name and address
                 you'll see there. I believe it's a strip
                 club.

STANLEY: Perhaps it would be better if I went
                 Miss Hepworth.

MISS HEPWORTH: No thank you Stanley, I think I shall probably find it an interesting experience. As far as I can recall I've never been inside a strip club before: I shall quite look forward to it. Well now, if you two would like to be getting on with trying to trace some of the others...

(FREDA is sitting in a factory snack bar with JANE EVANS, a dark-haired girl of 27.)

JANE: He goes off and leaves me with a baby - so what am I supposed to do after that?

FREDA: Are you getting maintenance?

JANE: Oh sure - on paper: a court order. Thirty-five bob a week when I can get it, which is when he feels like it. Somebody told me about Mrs Lawrence, I went to see her, she was nice. It seemed the best solution, if you knew the landlady at the digs where I am now -

FREDA: And how about your relatives?

JANE: We had a row, they didn't want me to marry him, they said he was no good. They were right. Well, I suppose I shall have to take a few days off now won't I, find somewhere else? The kid's only six months old, he's been with seven different people already. The only day nursery's eight miles away, a private one, it costs three guineas. (Sighs) It's not as though I stop at home all day and live on the National Assistance, I try and work for my living and -

FREDA: It might be better if you did, perhaps: a very young baby needs his mother.

JANE: What'd I get if I did? The rent and six

JANE: (Cont)	pounds odd for the two of us? At least I can earn thirteen here. It's not luxury even at that. (Quietly) It's easy for people like you to say it's wrong.
FREDA:	I haven't said that, as far as I'm aware. What I'm really trying to say is that we ought to work out some kind of long-term plan. (She scribbles on a piece of paper.) Look, here's my office number - will you give me a ring?
	(KATE NOLAN is very Irish and very pretty; she has auburn hair and dark blue eyes. She and STANLEY are talking in a side room off a ward in a hospital, at which she is a nurse.)
KATE:	Praise God Teresa's all right at least! But I don't know what to suggest for her - she's not my child you see, she really belongs to me sister.
STANLEY:	Perhaps you'd tell me where I can get in touch with her then.
KATE:	Well now it just so happens she's away to Dublin to see the family for a few days, and I'm looking after her for her.
STANLEY:	In that case will you give me her address in Dublin - it's very urgent we should get in touch with her.
KATE:	Oh no, I wouldn't want you to be going to all that bother now. You see, well can I be very honest with you? Me mother doesn't know anything at all about me sister having a child and that's a fact. And me brother he's going to be a priest too, so it'd be awful upsetting for her wouldn't it, and with her bad heart as well.
STANLEY:	Yes Miss Nolan, but my main concern is for the welfare of Teresa. Some-where has to be found for her to stay immediately.

KATE: Well she can't stay here with me that's for sure. I'm living in the nurse's home and Matron'd never allow that. She's a Protestant woman you see, very strict.

STANLEY: In that case we shall probably have to take Teresa into care. Would you have any objections?

KATE: Oh to be sure I would, I wouldn't like that to happen to her.

STANLEY: But as she's not your child -

KATE: Well - well you look a very understanding kind of a man to me. (Smiles) I told you a little fib, you see. Do you mind if I sit down for a minute, it's made me heart go like a clock it has... the shock of it you see. I felt it was Teresa, that maybe something had happened to her, you know.

STANLEY: Haven't you got any friends you could take her to temporarily?

KATE: No, only the man I'm... and you see he's a Protestant too. (Brightens) But I have got an auntie though. She lives over the other side of the town, I know she'd love to have her for a few days, she would. Yes that's it, that's what I'll do. I'm off duty at half past five now, will I be coming along to Mrs Lawrence's house then and take her off your hands?

STANLEY: That would do to begin with, yes. By the way Miss Nolan, had you been paying Mrs Lawrence?

KATE: Oh indeed I have, you couldn't expect her to be doing it for nothing now could you? Only... well I have been having a bit of a hard time just lately you know, and to be very honest with you it is a

KATE: Cont)	little while since I've actually given her anything. But I'll be settling it up with her soon enough; she's a very good woman you know, even though she's not a Catholic. Are you a Catholic yourself? (STANLEY shakes his head.) Oh well never mind. (KATE gives him a grin.) But if you ever get anything wrong with you and get brought in here, I'll look after you meself I will, and that's a promise! (As she goes out, STANLEY looks after her.) (FREDA is following VALERIE CHAPMAN into the basement room of a poorly furnished flat. VALERIE is 22, doll-faced, untidily dressed, and seven months pregnant. In the front room there is a twin-headed pram. VALERIE peeps inside it.)
VALERIE:	I've only just got them off.
FREDA:	How long has Laureen been staying with Mrs Lawrence?
VALERIE:	Oh, you know, off and on. (Yawns)
FREDA:	But how long has the arrangement actually been in existence?
VALERIE:	(Trying hard to understand.) Pardon?
FREDA:	How long has your baby been with Mrs Lawrence?
VALERIE:	(Thinks) A week, would it be that? Yes about a week.
FREDA:	And where was she before that?
VALERIE:	'Ere mostly - 'cept when she was wiv 'er - (Yawns) Ooh, sorry. (Nods across at the pram.) You wouldn't think they could be so quiet in the day would you, not the way they go on at night.

FREDA:	She's badly undernourished.
VALERIE:	What, you mean not fed? Yes I know. But she won't eat, I can't get 'er to eat, she cries and I'm tired and -
FREDA:	You've obviously got your hands full, Mrs Chapman. It might be an idea if we were to try and get you some help.
	(MICHAEL COLLINS comes in from another room. Long-haired, 22, off-putting in appearance: a typical layabout, one might think.)
VALERIE:	'S lady's from the welfare about Laureen.
FREDA:	Are you Mr Chapman, how do you do?
MICHAEL:	No: Mr Collins I am, Michael Collins.
FREDA:	(Turning to VALERIE.) Oh well Mrs Chapman as Laureen's your child -
MICHAEL:	She's my child as well. 'S just we're not married that's all. (Looking into the pram.) These's not mine though. (Laughs) Too noisy. Sleepin' all right now though ain't they Val? That's a relief, I can tell you. (To FREDA.) What's the matter wiv 'er then?
VALERIE:	That lady's been took ill and can't 'ave 'er no more.
MICHAEL:	We'll fetch 'er 'ere then.
VALERIE:	Aw Mike 'ow can we, not wiv them two carryin' on all the -
MICHAEL:	(Reasoning, kindly.) She's gorra sleep somewhere, love.
VALERIE:	The Welfare'll look after 'er.
MICHAEL:	But I mean she's our kid in't she? (To FREDA.) 'S not right is it, she needs 'er Mum? I've never liked 'er 'avin'

MICHAEL: (Cont)	to go to that woman. She doesn't eat, you know, but it's 'ard you see with those two and now (He nods at VALERIE.) know what I mean? And me bein' out of work an' all. Be all right on Monday though, doctor signed me off to go back then.
FREDA:	Laureen is your child, those two are not, and now - ?
MICHAEL:	Oh yes that's mine. (Waving vaguely towards the pram.) That's all finished with now. 'E was no good to 'er, was 'e love?
FREDA:	Is he paying something?
MICHAEL:	(Laughs) 'E's in the nick in't 'e? Well what do you think Val, I'll go and fetch our Laureen 'ere then eh?
FREDA:	If you can, that would certainly be the best, Mr Collins. I'll come and see you next week, then perhaps we can talk about getting some help for your... for Valerie - and think about finding somewhere better to live and -
MICHAEL:	Oh yeh, that'd be great if you could, eh Val? (Quietly, to FREDA.) She's 'ad a 'ard time yer know, but she's a good kid: you could find lots worse than 'er. (CUT TO a face on a poster of a half-caste girl wearing a feathered head-dress and nothing else. We see that it is hung in the passage entrance-way to a strip club in Soho. The legend beneath the poster reads 'Toto in toto'. Standing iron-faced in front of it is MISS HEPWORTH. As she goes into the strip club and pays her money, the proprietor lifts his eye-brows.) (CUT TO 'Toto" (STEPHANIE WARD)

in a wrap back-stage. She is 24, was
brought up in East London of mixed
parentage, and has a pronounced
cockney accent. Behind her a glimpse
of the stage and other dancing girls
going on and coming off: taped music.)

STEPHANIE: Well what the hell do you expect me to
do about it? I mean Lillian's not the
only one is she, I've got two others as
well and they're both in 'omes, I don't
want to put Lillian in one unless I 'ave
to, I was in one meself wasn't I so I
know what they're like.

MISS HEPWORTH: And what about Lillian's father, Miss
Ward?

STEPHANIE: 'Ow do you mean what about 'im? What
about 'im?

MISS HEPWORTH: Isn't he interested in her welfare?

STEPHANIE: Oh very funny I'm sure.

MISS HEPWORTH: You may think so Miss Ward, but I'm
afraid I don't, and I -

STEPHANIE: No well you wouldn't, would you? 'E
might be interested, yes 'e just might.
If I knew who 'e was.

MISS HEPWORTH: I see. Well what I'm trying to talk to
you about Miss Ward - (A dancer
squeezes between them.) difficult
though it is in these circumstances, is
what is going to happen to her? She
can't stay where she is.

STEPHANIE: Who says not?

MISS HEPWORTH: I say not, as head of the Children's
Department. So we can either take
Lillian into care, in which case you'll
be required to make regular payments
towards the cost; or else you'll have to
satisfy me that you've made a suitable
alternative arrangement.

STEPHANIE:	Oh charming! Anyone'd think she was your child, not mine, you interfering old -
MISS HEPWORTH:	In circumstances of this kind I have a statutory duty; and I shall if necessary obtain a court order to say the child is in need of care and protection. She is also seriously under-fed.
STEPHANIE:	Well 'oo's fault's that? I'm payin' 'er enough.
MISS HEPWORTH:	How much are you paying her?
STEPHANIE:	Two quid a bloody week! If you can't feed a child on that -
MISS HEPWORTH:	And when did you last pay her?
STEPHANIE:	Last week - well - well a couple of weeks ago, I can't manage it every -
MISS HEPWORTH:	You'd better come and see me at my office Miss Ward - here's my address. I shall require a great deal of convincing that your child wouldn't be better off in care.
STEPHANIE:	Oh will you? Well you try that and I'll bring 'er to live with me, somewhere out of your -
MISS HEPWORTH:	It will still be my duty to inform the Children's Department in which ever area you are living. (Softly) Miss Ward, I've really no wish to be on these terms at all with you, I'd sooner discuss it in a friendly way. Can't we -
STEPHANIE:	Friendly! You come in 'ere talking about court orders and then you say you want to be friendly - you've got a nerve, 'aven't you? Well you can just eff off! (She flings off her wrap and stalks towards the stage.)
	(The face of a Nigerian baby: it is in

MRS WATTS' arms in one of the rooms at Lyndhurst Avenue.)

MRS WATTS: Eh, you're lovely, yes you are, aren't you, eh? I don't know, some people - 'ow can they do it, leavin' their kids all day in a place like this?

STANLEY: I suppose if they could think of something better, or find it, they would. People drift into this kind of situation because circumstances have got on top of them. I must say community services for unsupported mothers with children are not exactly high up on the list of expenditures of local authorities. We need more day nurseries, more trained social workers, more organisation, more awareness -

MRS WATTS: Yes? Go on.

STANLEY: Sorry - I should have stood for the local council. I'll go and make some custard for their tea instead.

(JOHN BLACK is coming out of the front door of MRS MILLS' house and down the garden path. He gets into his car and drives off. Over a series of shots of him driving, he is recollecting the interview he has just had with MRS MILLS. We hear it in voice-over throughout the next sequence, and occasionally see shots of MRS MILLS, a plain middle-aged woman.)

JOHN BLACK: Mrs Mills? Good afternoon, I'm from The Gazette.

MRS MILLS: Why have you come to see me... why have you come to see me...

JOHN BLACK: I've been doing rather a lot of research Mrs Mills...

MRS MILLS: Go away... please leave me alone...
               go away.

JOHN BLACK: Help you Mrs Mills... readers rally
               round, they often do...

MRS MILLS: Not for me... no, not for me... go
               away and leave me alone, please...

JOHN BLACK: I won't use your name...

MRS MILLS: My husband at sea, an engineer, two
               lovely children, a nice home... last
               year... Australia, New Zealand...
               and only once, having a drink with the
               husband of a friend... before she was
               born I tried everything I knew...

JOHN BLACK: Wouldn't it have been better to have told
               him, Mrs Mills?

MRS MILLS: A proud man, a good man, but he
               couldn't forgive, he wouldn't if he ever
               ... and what about you, if it were you,
               would you...

               (In the hospital ward, MRS LAWRENCE
               is being bedded down for the night. A
               NURSE's hand turns out the light over
               her bed.)

               (At Lyndhurst Avenue too the bedroom
               lights are going off, but lights are still
               on downstairs. In the kitchen
               STANLEY is pouring tea for MRS
               WATTS and FREDA. FREDA sits, a
               little less neat than usual.)

FREDA: Christ, what a day! Give me a
               cigarette, Stanley.

MRS WATTS: 'Ello, is that one of 'em cryin'?

FREDA: Sit down Mrs Watts, sit down - Betty's
               up there, she'll deal with it. (Takes
               out her notebook.) Well now, what's
               the score? (Ticks them off.) She's

FREDA: (Cont)	gone, she's gone, that one's gone - that was one of yours Stanley? (She passes over her list.)
STANLEY:	(Looking down the list.) Yes. And Miss Nolan's been, the Percivals have been - a right funny lot they were too, very hoity toity, the old man's a big guy on the Council or something, there's a lot going on there, don't know the details yet.
FREDA:	(Taking back the list and adding up.) One, two, three... only seven left. I'll stop with you here tonight Mrs Watts.
MRS WATTS:	I can manage you know if you'd rather -
FREDA:	I've nothing else to do except go home and watch the telly, and I've no food in the flat anyway. Well Stanley, are you on your way home then?
STANLEY:	Yes, I think I will, my wife will be wondering. Good night Mrs Watts; see you in the morning Freda, good night. (He goes.)
MRS WATTS:	Nice man Mr Maxwell, isn't he?
FREDA:	Yes. (Pause) Would you like another cup of tea?
	(It is morning. MRS LAWRENCE is being woken up in the hospital, and given a cup of tea by a NURSE. The curtains are being pulled back around her bed.)
	(And at the windows of Lyndhurst Avenue. The clock on the mantlepiece in the kitchen shows soon after nine o'clock. MISS HEPWORTH is already there in the kitchen with FREDA and STANLEY.)
MISS HEPWORTH:	I'm still very concerned at the lack of

49

MISS HEPWORTH: (Cont)	information we have about some of them, we don't seem to know anything at all about -
STANLEY:	It's more complicated than we thought. She wasn't just an unregistered baby minder, she seems to have been an unofficial temporary foster mother too.
FREDA:	It was all so haphazard - all right, she's been stupid and she's taken on far too many, but people have taken advantage of her. 'Mrs Lawrence'll look after it for a bit until we get something sorted out'. That seems to have been the general attitude.
STANLEY:	How did you get on at the strip club, Miss Hepworth?
MISS HEPWORTH:	If it was one of your cases Stanley and I was supervising it, I should describe it as 'a total failure of communication'. I'm afraid I over-estimated my -
	(A look of blank astonishment on MISS HEPWORTH's face as she sees who is standing in the kitchen doorway: STEPHANIE WARD.)
STEPHANIE:	(Embarrassed, placatory.) 'Morning, I - I thought I'd better - well I'm going to take 'er to my sister's for a bit, is that OK?
MISS HEPWORTH:	(Who can't help smiling with relief.) Good morning Miss Ward. Miss Wills, would you be kind enough to -
FREDA:	(Rising, smiling.) Yes of course, good morning, if you'd like to come in the other room -
	(As FREDA and STEPHANIE go into the hall BETTY LAWRENCE is coming down the stairs carrying a baby she has been dressing.)

BETTY:	Oh 'ello Steph, 'ow are you, 'ow's it goin'?
STEPHANIE:	'Ello Bett, not so bad, 'ow's your Mum?
BETTY:	Not too bad they said this morning. Come for your Lillian, I thought you wasn't comin' till Saturday?
STEPHANIE:	Well - you know how it is.
BETTY:	She's in there, she's fine, see you Steph.
STEPHANIE:	Yeh, see you Bett.

(STEPHANIE goes into the back room with FREDA following her. MRS WATTS is tidying around, and smiles at her. STEPHANIE crosses the room to where two babies, one white and one coloured, are lying side by side in a cot. She picks up the white one.)

Come on love, you've got to go to your auntie's for a bit. (To MRS WATTS and FREDA.) Thanks very much for... well, come on then darlin'. (She goes out.)

MRS WATTS:	(As she and FREDA look at the remaining coloured baby.) Well I'll be ... then 'oo the 'ell does.... ?

(MR LOW is a large, amiable and softly-spoken Nigerian. He is sitting on a sofa in a small and poorly furnished room next to his WIFE.)

MR LOW:	Evelina is a student of law, so to keep us going I am a road sweeper for the Corporation. Soon, next year perhaps, she will pass her final examination, then we have more money and everything is OK.
FREDA:	It's not really very good for your little girl, Mr Low, to leave her more or less permanently with somebody else.

MR LOW: Oh but we see her regularly once a month without fail. It is expensive to travel such a long way, but we never miss. We take her to the park, buy her ice-cream, some clothes, what ever she needs, we give her a treat. It is better than to have her here in this not very nice house, dirty, smelly, all the people, you will have seen for yourself. With Mrs Lawrence she grows up with nice English children, so when she is a big girl she does not feel a stranger so much in this country, it is her home. We have had to try very hard to find an English house for her, and so we are lucky. We are happy, our daughter is happy, everything is very good. But I think sometimes English people are funny - do you not want integration?

(TERRY ALLEN brings STANLEY MAXWELL into the living room of a brand new council flat. TERRY is a brash, cheerful, curly haired young man of about 21.)

TERRY: (Shouts) Linda! There's someone 'ere from the welfare about Chrissie! Linda!

(LINDA ALLEN, also about 21, and pretty, comes in, wrapping herself in a bath towel.)

LINDA: Gawd strewf, carn I 'ave a barf in peace wivout you bawlin' the - oh sorry I thought it'd be a lady, it usually is.

TERRY: This geyser's come to tell us Mrs doin's can't 'ave Chrissie no more.

LINDA: Carn 'ave 'er, why not? I carn 'ave 'er 'ere.

STANLEY: Do you have other children, Mrs Allen?

LINDA:	'Ang on, I on'y jus' come out've borstal, an' I? I 'ad 'er while I was in there. (Giggles) Terry come on a visit.
STANLEY:	Didn't you want to keep her, when you came out?
LINDA:	Yeh, but it's not all that easy is it; any'ow I can't stick 'er just now, she's got that dirty thing with 'er eyes, always playin' with 'erself, I've smacked 'er and smacked 'er but it makes no difference.
STANLEY:	Why don't you take her to the doctor?
LINDA:	(Nodding towards TERRY.) 'E's not paid 'is stamps 'as 'e? Any'ow, I got some ointment stuff off-of a girl in the flats, 'er kid 'ad it too, only 'is cleared up.
STANLEY:	She'll have to be taken to hospital, she needs attention urgently.
LINDA:	Oh that's good then, 'cos that's the best place for 'er innit Terry?
STANLEY:	Mrs Allen, she's your child and she's been badly neglected.
TERRY:	'Ere now watch it mate, we carn 'elp it can we, we're tryin' to 'ave 'er. Just as soon as we gerrour own 'ouse, aren't we Linda? I mean the council give us this to start wiv like, but it's not a proper 'ouse is it? I mean yer need a 'ouse if yer've gotta kid doncher? 'Ere, p'raps you could do somethin' to 'elp us?
STANLEY:	If you're not prepared to have her with you, we shall take her into care -
TERRY:	Wotcher mean, not prepared - we've just said we will ant we?
STANLEY:	You'll have to pay for the cost of her upkeep. Are you working?

53

TERRY: Yeh, 'course - me an' a mate gorrour
own business, paintin' and decoratin'.
Only you know what the wevver's been
like. (He smacks LINDA's bottom.)
Go on now, don't you 'ang about Linda,
you'll catch yer deff.

(LINDA goes off back to the bathroom,
and TERRY turns confidentially to
STANLEY, shepherding him towards
the flat door.)

You know 'ow it is guv wiv these kids,
not long art've borstal and back on the -
(Gesture to indicate hyperdermic.) know
wharra mean? Doin' me best wiv 'er -
but it takes time, mate, dunnit? Nice
toys and that do they 'ave in them
children's 'omes? I'll tell yer, I do, I
admire you people, I think you've got a
very difficult job, straight up.

(By this time he has got STANLEY out
of the door and has shut it behind him.
We see that STANLEY is outside a flat
door on the third floor of a block of
council flats. He sets off along the
balcony and down the several staircases.
At the bottom he cannons into JOHN
BLACK.)

JOHN BLACK: Sorry! Oh - it's you. Look - could I
have a word with you?

STANLEY: No. (He walks off.)

(MR BANCROFT is a shirt-sleeved
pipe-smoking off-duty railway ticket-
collector. He stands in front of the
fire place in the small sitting room of
his home. In the background his wife
MRS BANCROFT never gets any chance
to express an opinion.)

MR BANCROFT: What's it got to do with you people, why do you have to start pushing your noses in?

MRS BANCROFT: Fred -

MR BANCROFT: Shut up. Well?

FREDA: I'd like to know what your daughter Barbara wants to do about her baby, Mr Bancroft.

MR BANCROFT: I don't know yet: we shall have to think.

FREDA: Could I have a word with Barbara?

MR BANCROFT: No you couldn't. (Pause) She's not here. (Longer pause.) She's at school.

FREDA: Is the child's father paying for -

MR BANCROFT: His parents are. He went to prison for it. She's only fourteen.

FREDA: And how old is he?

MR BANCROFT: Eighteen, nineteen.

FREDA: And you say he went to prison for -

MR BANCROFT: Three months. And if you want my opinion, 'e got off lightly. Well - anything else?

MRS BANCROFT: Fred, can't we -

MR BANCROFT: No we can't, why don't you keep your mouth shut? Always sticking your oar in. Didn't I say all along adoption'd be the best?

FREDA: I'd like to have a talk with the father, anyway.

MR BANCROFT: That's up to you: I can't stop you. If you do, you can make one thing plain - I haven't altered my opinion. There'll be no marriage, not next year, the year after, or any other time. And that's flat - so you make it clear to young Peter Unwin, will you?

(In her office FREDA is talking to
PETER UNWIN, a quiet, good looking
boy of 19, until recently a college
student.)

PETER: And I don't suppose he will ever change
                his mind.

FREDA: Do you still see Barbara?

PETER: It's not all that easy. When I came out
                of the detention centre I left college and
                got a job in a shop. The only chance I
                get of seeing her is on Wednesday's
                when it's half day, I wait for her after
                school and we go in the park for a walk
                on her way home.

FREDA: What's your mother and father's
                attitude?

PETER: They've been very good. My father
                wanted me to stay at college, he said
                he'd pay for... but it is my child, so I
                think I ought to pay. Barbara and me
                are saving up as much as we can, when
                she's old enough we're going to apply to
                the court for permission to get
                married. I shan't ever give her up.

FREDA: Her father wants her to have the child
                adopted.

PETER: Yes I know - but I've got some rights,
                because there's an affiliation order.
                I've always admitted it was my child
                right from the start. Funny, isn't it -
                if I hadn't, I wouldn't have got sent
                away for it.

                (MRS LAWRENCE in hospital is now
                much better. She is sitting up in bed
                and having a cup of tea. FREDA is at
                the bedside.)

MRS LAWRENCE: Oh Miss I am sorry I am, causing all

MRS LAWRENCE: (Cont)	that trouble for everyone. But it's hard to turn people away when they're in a mess isn't it? They're such lovely kiddies you know, all of them, you do get fond of them, I really was trying to do my best but it all got -
FREDA:	But you see young babies need more than just feeding and keeping clean, Mrs Lawrence, they need individual attention, being picked up and played with and talked to - far more than you could manage on your own.
MRS LAWRENCE:	Yes they do, don't they? But it's not easy for the mothers is it, I mean if they want to try and do their best to keep their baby, what are they supposed to do?
FREDA:	I'd be the last person to say that community services for unsupported mothers are all they might be.
MRS LAWRENCE:	(Gloomily) Shall I get into a lot of trouble Miss?
FREDA:	The only honest answer I can give at this stage is I don't know. Fortunately none of them has been injured or neglected or starved - though they could have had a better diet. But I know money was not always paid when it should have been... I think a great deal depends on the future, Mrs Lawrence.
MRS LAWRENCE:	Oh I've learned my lesson Miss, I have, I certainly have. I won't never get into that sort of situation again, believe you me I won't. When I get 'ome I'm just going to take things very quiet and easy for a long while.

(MRS LAWRENCE is out of hospital. She has been out to get a packet of tea, which she carries in her string shopping

bag as she walks home down Lyndhurst
Avenue and turns into the gate of 106.
At the front door is a GIRL who is just
going away after getting no reply; she
has a baby in her arms.

We do not hear the dialogue between her
and MRS LAWRENCE but we see MRS
LAWRENCE look fondly at the baby,
tickle its cheek, smile, and then regret-
fully shake her head. Sadly the GIRL
starts to walk away down the path. MRS
LAWRENCE at her front door watches
her go, conflicting emotions on her face.
Finally she can bear it no longer.)

MRS LAWRENCE: (Calls) Eh, I say! Just a minute...

(The GIRL turns and looks back. MRS
LAWRENCE has opened her front door
with her key, and beckons her to come
inside. The GIRL starts back up the
path with her baby, towards the smiling,
welcoming MRS LAWRENCE.)

(Over this the final credits come up,
and additionally:-

The author gratefully acknowledges the
help he has received from a number of
Local Authority Children's Departments,
and from the National Council for the
Unmarried Mother and Her Child. The
names of persons concerned have been
altered, and so have identifiable details:
but all the case histories in this play
have occurred within the past twelve
months.)

FINISH
————

Chariot of Fire

For Irene Shubick

CHARIOT OF FIRE

This play, performed twice on television, is about
the unmentionables in our society - child molesters.
It describes, without prejudice, the circumstances
of one such case, the plight of all those involved and
the great efforts of the welfare services who seek to
help the convicted in the most difficult circumstances.

CHARIOT OF FIRE was first shown on BBC-1 in May 1970, and repeated in 1971.

Shelley Mitchell. ... ROSEMARY LEACH

Stanley Wood ...... JIMMY GARDNER

John Mitchell ...... CHARLES TINGWELL

Mrs Lee .... BETTY COOPER

It was produced by Irene Shubik and directed by James Ferman

CAST

POLICE MOTOR PATROLMAN BRADLEY

SERGEANT COOPER

'SPIDER' WEBB

MICHAEL STARKIE, aged 11

GORDON ASHMAN, aged 13

ALAN EVANS, aged 13

STEPHEN RUSSELL, aged 12

MARVIN HURST, aged 12

JOHN MITCHELL

MARK MITCHELL

ROBERT MITCHELL

MRS LEE

SHELLEY MITCHELL

DAVID LINCOLN

STANLEY WOOD

GARFIELD)
)   CID
WORTLEY   )

t is nearly 10 o'clock on a Saturday evening in winter, and
.n the dark a chariot of fire is trundling down a slope of
waste ground. Flaring, smoking, smouldering: at first we
:an hardly make out what it is. A battered wooden fruit-
:rate, tied onto a set of old pram-wheels, and half-filled with
:ubbish and scraps of newspaper. Gathering momentum, and
with the draught of its progress making the contents sputter
erratically into flame the chariot rolls on: up a short slope,
down a long one, trundling over level ground, continuing
across a pavement and out into the road-way, mounting the
kerb of the pavement at the other side, and coming to a halt
at last with a crash and a shower of sparks against the wall of
a building. As it goes, the title comes up:-

CHARIOT OF FIRE

A police patrol car is coming along the street. It stops, and
its crew get out to investigate this object which only moments
before shot ahead of them across the road. Police motor
patrolmen BRADLEY and SERGEANT COOPER, both peak-
capped and uniformed. BRADLEY pushes his cap back on his
head, stands with his hands on his hips, prods the fruit-crate
cautiously with his boot. COOPER, the car driver, has
followed him: he frowns distastefully at it, rubs his chin with
his thumb and forefinger. COOPER turns, looks back across
the other side of the street: BRADLEY's eyes follow his.
Waste ground, and distant and higher up the rear of a sweet
factory: dimly perceivable there, flickers of light and moving
shadows. None too pleased they exchanged glances and nods.
'Oh well, I suppose we'll have to, come on then'; and they set
off on the climb up to it.

Behind the sweet factory is a piece of ground littered with oil
drums and empty packing cases, enclosed on three sides by
walls. Here, a group of boys, aimless and inconsequent:
some lounging about, some throwing stones, one or two
smoking, a few trying to keep alight a small fire they have
made.

The oldest and tallest is 'SPIDER' WEBB, 15, gangly, thin-
faced and long haired: the youngest and smallest is
MICHAEL STARKIE, 11, chubby and moon-faced. The others

are between them in age and size: GORDON ASHMAN, 13:
ALAN EVANS, 13: STEPHEN RUSSELL, 12: and MARVIN
HURST, 12.

It is 'SPIDER' who first sees COOPER and BRADLEY as the
appear. His quick gesture and hissed 'Heh!' warns the other
who all freeze.

COOPER:	(Menacing, quiet.) All right, what's all this then? (Nobody says anything.) Well, come on someone, let's 'ave you: what are you up to?
	(All the boys look to 'SPIDER' to do the talking. He is not over-awed by the police; cautious, cool, waiting to assess why they are here.)
SPIDER:	Nothin'.
	(BRADLEY switches on his torch, and pinpoints SPIDER with it.)
BRADLEY:	I might've known you'd be mixed up in it
SPIDER:	In what, I'm not doin' no 'arm.
BRADLEY:	You couldn't do anything else but 'arm you couldn't.
	(The smallest boy, MICHAEL STARKIE, has been trying to creep away unobserved round the edge of the wall; COOPER grabs him, shining his torch in his face.)
COOPER:	Oh no you don't! Where do you think you're off to? What's your name?
MICHAEL:	Please Sir, Michael Starkie, Sir. (A puff of cigarette smoke comes out of his mouth when he speaks.)
COOPER:	Smokin' at your age. All right please sir Michael Starkie sir, well what are you up to?

MICHAEL:	Nothin' Sir, honestly.
COOPER:	'Ow about you then, Spider?
SPIDER:	'Ow about me what?
COOPER:	Know anythin' about it?
SPIDER:	(Contemptuously) Do me a favour, Cooper.
COOPER:	Sergeant Cooper to you, Webb. Where's all your friends of your own age tonight then?
SPIDER:	(A glint in his eye, cool but not ingratiating.) Told not to knock about wiv me own mates, wan I?
COOPER:	(A humourless smile.) So you were. Glad to see you takin' notice.
BRADLEY:	All right then, come on then, which one of you did it?
SPIDER:	What you on about, what're we supposed to 'ave -
BRADLEY:	Sent that thing flyin' down into the road on fire, scratched that gentleman's car, nearly knocked down that old lady. (Pause) Well come on, 'oo was it?
SPIDER:	(Genuinely puzzled.) What? (Suddenly it dawns on him what must have happened. He turns on GORDON ASH-MAN.) You, yer stupid git, that old box thing on wheels.
GORDON:	What you talkin' about, I only give it a kick down - (He looks round, and of course it is no longer there. He turns to BRADLEY, aghast.) You mean it went all the... ?
SPIDER:	Stupid nit.
GORDON:	I didn't do it. It was 'im frew the match in it. (To MARVIN.) You great steamin' -

MARVIN:	You bloody liar, it was you that was tranna knock everyone else -
GORDON:	Oh no it bleedin' wasn't, it was you -
COOPER:	Shut your mouths, the pair of you! That the language they learn you at school, is it? (In the ensuing silence, he slowly undoes his breast-pocket, and takes out his note book.) Right then: we'll start with all your names and addresses, shall we?
SPIDER:	(Cool, head slightly on one side.) Bloke 'oo's car got scratched still down there, is 'e? And 'ow about the old lady - sent 'er off to 'ospital in an ambulance, 'ave you?
BRADLEY:	There's one name and address we shan't need to ask, isn't there?
COOPER:	Eh! What's that?
	(MICHAEL STARKIE has dropped something on the ground behind his back. COOPER retrieves a nearly full packet of cigarettes.)
	Where'd you get these?
MICHAEL:	They was given me. By a man, a feller.
COOPER:	A feller? What feller? What was 'is name then, Santa Claus? You pinched 'em, didn't you?
MICHAEL:	No 'e did, 'e give them me, honest.
COOPER:	All right then, what was 'is name?
MICHAEL:	Stanley.
COOPER:	(Still disbelieving him.) Stanley what?
MICHAEL:	I don't know 'is other name: just Stanley.
	('SPIDER' whistles softly and tunelessly through his teeth. He leans back against the wall, thumbs in his pockets, idly

flicking at a stone with his foot, watching the policemen from under narrowed eye-lids, knowing the effect what he says will have on them.)

SPIDER: (Quietly) Stanley... Wood.

(A silence, a stillness. BRADLEY jerks up his head and looks at 'SPIDER': COOPER looks at BRADLEY: 'SPIDER' carefully watches them both.)

COOPER: (To MICHAEL.) Was that 'is name, son?

MICHAEL: It might be, I dunno. But 'e did give them to me, you ask 'im! Honest I didn't pinch 'em... (Looks helplessly from one policeman to the other, unable to under-stand what is happening. He has no comprehension of the new element in the atmosphere.)

COOPER: Earlier on tonight, was this? (MICHAEL nods.) Round at 'is place, were you?

MICHAEL: Yes, we was all there. They must 'ave seen 'im give them me, didn't yer? (He turns to the others.)

COOPER: (Quietly, politely.) Come on son, you just come over 'ere a minute and let's 'ave a chat. (Puts a fatherly arm round MICHAEL's shoulder and shepherds him away. He continues to talk as they go. Quietly.) An' what were you doin' when you were round there?

MICHAEL: Just playin' games, Sir.

COOPER: Oh yes? An' what sort of games would they be, then?

(The interior of the MITCHELL's living room, that evening. Like any other civilised man JOHN MITCHELL is watching 'Match of the Day' this Saturday evening. On the television screen a shot of a Chelsea game, with the commentator's voice over.)

JOHN: Oh my God, for Christ's sake, why don't you pass, you -

(JOHN is in casual clothes. He is totally engrossed in the game and keeping up a loud running commentary to himself. When his son MARK, aged 9, comes in in pyjamas and dressing gown and crosses his line of vision, you'd think JOHN was in the packed crowd on the terraces.)

Mark, for God's sake! Get out of the way

MARK: Is that Charlie Cooke, Daddy?

JOHN: (Never taking his eyes off the scren.) No Cooke's injured, he's not playing.

MARK: Did Chelsea win?

JOHN: Shut up!

MARK: Have they scored yet?

JOHN: Look, it's long past your bed time - oh no you idiot, pass to Osgood!

(JOHN's other son, ROBERT, aged 7 and also in pyjamas comes in and climbs up on the back of his father's chair to watch.

ROBERT: Go on Charlie, good old Charlie, go on!

MARK: (Sarcastically) It's not Charlie, you twit, he's injured, that's Hudson.

ROBERT: No it's not, it's Charlie Cooke, isn't it Daddy?

JOHN: No it's not, I've just told you he's - Robert, what the blazes are you doing still up? (Shouting with exasperation.) Shelley! Shelley!

(But it is not his wife, it is his mother-in-law MRS LEE who comes into the room. She is 60, small, a bit vague, not short of money, neatly dressed and trim.)

MRS LEE: She'll be in in a moment dear, she's just bringing the coffee.

JOHN: What on earth's she doing letting these kids roam around at this time, they ought to have been in bed hours - oh shoot, you idiot! Oh Shelley, do please do something about them, will you?

(Bringing in a tray with coffee on it, SHELLEY MITCHELL, his wife, is good looking, quietly spoken, and about 30. A wife and mother, but with a strong streak of her own individuality which she has preserved throughout ten years of marriage without having to struggle to do it. JOHN's respect for her has never changed, nor his love. Any unhappiness or dissatisfaction she feels comes from her nature rather than her situation. Because he feels things less, JOHN is more content with material possessions, of which the house is but one indication of his success in business.)

SHELLEY: Come on Robert and Mark. I'll read you a story in bed.

ROBERT: No Mummy, please let's stay up and watch this.

JOHN: Certainly not! Shelley, do -

(Out in the hall the telephone rings. SHELLEY is off to answer it in a flash. In the hall, she whips up the receiver.)

SHELLEY: Hello? (Pause: disappointment on her face.) Oh, hello Peter. Fine thanks, yes, he's here, I'll get him. (She puts the

72

SHELLEY: (Cont)	receiver down on the hall table and goes back into the living room.) John, it's Peter for you.
JOHN:	Sod! (Exasperated, he gets up and switches off the television set, much to his sons' disappointment. He goes out into the hall.)
MRS LEE:	(To SHELLEY.) You sit and have your coffee dear, I'll read to them, you look awfully tired.
SHELLEY:	(Dispiritedly) Really, would you mind?
MRS LEE:	Not a bit, I shall enjoy it. Robert, come on, Mark - let's see if we can find some thing nice shall we? (She takes the boys off upstairs.)
	(SHELLEY sits on the settee, pours out two cups of coffee. She lights a cigarette, glances at her wrist watch, taps her fingers on the arm of the settee frowns, draws hard on her cigarette.
	JOHN comes back, flops in his chair, drinks his coffee, picks up a motoring magazine, and only after a while glances across at SHELLEY.)
JOHN:	Something the matter?
SHELLEY:	(Quietly) No. (She glances at her watch again, and taps her fingers.)
JOHN:	Peter wants me to play a round of golf in the morning, so I can drop mother off at the station on the way.
SHELLEY:	(After a pause.) John, would you mind very much, I was wondering if I could have the car in the morning?
JOHN:	Yes, sure. Drop mother off at the station, me at the club, and then you and the kids can go -

SHELLEY:	I shall have to go on my own. What I really meant was could you stop at home and look after the children?
JOHN:	(Mildly) Darling, I've just said I've fixed up to play golf with Peter.
SHELLEY:	I'm terribly sorry John, but I simply must go out in the morning.
JOHN:	(Puts down the magazine: still mildly.) Well I suppose there are husbands who might start imagining things. Why particularly tomorrow morning?
SHELLEY:	He didn't 'phone at eight o'clock.
JOHN:	Sorry love - who didn't?
SHELLEY:	Stanley.
JOHN:	He'll probably 'phone tomorrow then, or you can ring him.
SHELLEY:	He hasn't got a 'phone. John, this is the first Saturday night in seven months he hasn't rung precisely at eight o'clock.
JOHN:	Well he's gone out for a drink, met a friend or something.
SHELLEY:	No. 'Saturday's the worst night, the really lonely one'.
JOHN:	Pardon?
SHELLEY:	Something he said once.
JOHN:	Oh Shelley relax, don't worry. He's done all right so far hasn't he? That night he turned up here drunk with nowhere to live, I'd never have believed he'd stay out for a -
SHELLEY:	That wasn't Stanley, that was Billy Green.
JOHN:	Oh. I'm sorry darling, I can't always remember the difference. Stanley... which one is he then? No, don't tell me, I'll get it in a minute. He's not the chap who married the - no, that was George

JOHN: (Cont)	wasn't it? (Thinks) Hm. Have you told me a lot about him?
SHELLEY:	No John. As a matter of fact, I've never told you anything about Stanley at all. (Flash back. A year or two before, SHELLEY is in the office of a Prison Governor, DAVID LINCOLN. In his late forties, LINCOLN is young for his position in charge of a large local prison He is not officious: amiable but not hearty, firm but not inflexible. A reliable upholder of a system, but he is not blind to its shortcomings. He is leaning forward lighting a cigarette for her.) Thank you. You didn't ask me to come for a polite chat, I'm sure?
LINCOLN:	No. (Pause) You've been one of our associates for how long now Mrs Mitchell three years is it? (SHELLEY nods.) And how many men have you got on your hands at the moment?
SHELLEY:	Two.
LINCOLN:	Have you possibly got the time to take on another? He won't be released for eight or nine months yet, so you'd have quite a while to get to know him.
SHELLEY:	Tell me something about him.
LINCOLN:	(Picking up a folder from the desk in front of him.) Age fifty-nine, single, seven previous convictions. Now serving four and a half years. Jobs when out - clerk, baker's roundsman, milkman, shop assistant, van driver. No relatives, no contacts, no letters, no visits. (Glances at his watch.) Would you like to see him? (SHELLEY looks puzzled.) Go and look out of that window over there.

(SHELLEY goes over to one of the
windows of LINCOLN's office. We hear
him talking in voice-over as we see what
she sees. In the prison exercise yard
below, about two hundred men are
walking round. Some are chatting in
groups, others walking on their own.
One or two prison officers stand, bored,
keeping an eye on them.)

LINCOLN: The men are exercising. Can you see
over at the far side of the yard, a man
walking up and down on his own?

SHELLEY: Yes.

(The camera closes in on this MAN.
Small, thin, frail: we do not see his face,
only that he is separate from all the
others.)

LINCOLN: That's how he spends the exercise period
- on his own.

SHELLEY: What's his name?

LINCOLN: Stanley Wood.

SHELLEY: And what's he in for?

LINCOLN: The one crime you don't talk about - not
even to other prisoners.

(We are now back in LINCOLN's office.)

You don't talk about it because you're
scared. And for good reason - plenty
would give you a good going over if they
knew. A prisoner within a prison. He's
in for indecent assault on small boys.

SHELLEY: (Slight pause.) Do you think he'd accept
an associate?

LINCOLN: He might. If he took to the person
concerned. But that wouldn't be certain,
and it wouldn't be easy for them. (He

LINCOLN:
(Cont)

looks back at the file.) First conviction not until he was thirty. Six months, twelve months, eighteen months, two years, two years, eight years, and now four and a half years. Nineteen and a half years out of the last thirty. Health good, intelligence within the normal IQ range. Has been in a job nearly every time he's been convicted; and his last employer gave him a testimonial as honest, hard working, and reliable. Permanent address, offences always take place there, and he pleads guilty every time. Six boys involved on this sentence, eight charges the time before. So it's gone on, the same pattern, about a year between sentences.

SHELLEY:

Is he having any treatment?

LINCOLN:

No. So far, when anyone's tried to raise the subject, he says he doesn't feel the need to do it anymore, and he knows he'll be all right when he goes out. He doesn't want to talk about it - he's so ashamed of it, he doesn't even want to think about it.

SHELLEY:

And what are his chances?

LINCOLN:

Seven previous convictions, well known in the locality where he lives, a sitting target any time for boys who are not too particular about what they do to get a bit of pocket money... what would you think?

SHELLEY:

What gives you the idea I might have any success with him?

LINCOLN:

You could spend more time on him, for one thing. It mightn't work, but I think it's worth a try. If he doesn't ever find anyone he can talk to, someone he can trust, there's no hope at all. Sometimes I think he's just waiting to die. To begin with I'm sure he'll think you're a psychiatrist that we're trying to land him with.

SHELLEY: (Slight laugh.) I'm sure he won't - once
           he's seen my home and the children.

LINCOLN: How many have you?

SHELLEY: Two very noisy and very badly behaved
           little boys, one eight and the other six.

LINCOLN: His offences are always with the pre-
           pubertal age group, seven to about
           twelve or thirteen.

SHELLEY: (Pause) Just as a matter of interest,
           what exactly is 'indecent assault'?

           (End of flash back. We are back in
           SHELLEY's sitting room.)

JOHN: Well are you going to tell me anything?

           (SHELLEY is about to speak, but MRS
           LEE comes into the room.)

MRS LEE: (To SHELLEY.) They're waiting for you
           to go up and kiss them good-night.

SHELLEY: Yes all right. I'm afraid the coffee's
           getting a bit cold. (She goes out.)

           (MRS LEE pours herself some coffee,
           and sits.)

MRS LEE: She looks tired, is there anything wrong?

JOHN: Oh you know Shelley, always worrying.
           Just that one of her prisoners hasn't
           'phoned when he should have done -
           something and nothing, I suppose.

           (CUT TO the interior of STANLEY
           WOOD's bungalow-shack at night. A hand
           pushes open the door. BRADLEY and
           SERGEANT COOPER enter. Pitch
           darkness within; BRADLEY's torch beam
           finds the light switch by the door, and he
           switches it on. A low-powered bulb and

a cheap shade hanging from the middle
of the ceiling. The camera pans round:
the room is cluttered and untidy, but
clean. An old upright piano with a
framed photograph on the top: an old
book case and display cabinet with a few
ornaments; arm chairs, and a settee
which has seen better days.

Fully clothed and torpid with drink,
STANLEY is lying spread-eagled, face
down, on the bed along one wall of the
room. An empty VP Wine bottle has
dropped from his hand onto the floor.
Scattered around are a couple of
crumpled paper hats, a jig-saw puzzle
box with the pieces spilling out, and a
child's plastic aeroplane. BRADLEY's
foot crunches on it as he walks over.

There is nothing remarkable about
STANLEY WOOD: an inconspicuous
looking man with thin grey hair and
watery eyes, in a cheap plain suit.

BRADLEY and COOPER know this man
well. They have great distaste for him,
but they know he never gives any trouble
when arrested. BRADLEY stands at the
foot of the bed and shakes STANLEY's
shoulder.)

BRADLEY: Wood! All right Wood, wake up!

(STANLEY mumbles, opens his eyes,
tries to focus on the metal buttons on the
blue tunic just in front of his nose.
Slowly he lifts his head and looks up.)

All right, come on, put your shoes on,
we're taking you down the station for
questioning.

(STANLEY lowers his head: slowly,
protectingly, his arms come up and fold
over at the back of it. He starts to
tremble. COOPER shakes him roughly.)

COOPER:　　(Through his teeth.) Come on you
bastard, we haven't got all night.

(But SHELLEY has. She is lying awake
in bed. On the table by the side of it the
alarm clock shows it is nearly three
o'clock in the morning.)

JOHN:　　(Sleepily) You still awake? Why don't
you take a pill?

SHELLEY:　　I have done.

JOHN:　　(Still sleepily.) If he hasn't 'phoned by
half past ten in the morning, you take the
car, I'll ring up Peter. Only try and get
some sleep now darling. (Yawns)

(SHELLEY comes down stairs. MARK
and ROBERT are playing in the sitting
room.)

SHELLEY:　　Be good for Daddy. I'll be back for lunch
time.

(SHELLEY is driving through the
deserted Sunday suburbs of London. It is
raining. As she drives, she thinks.)

(Flash back. STANLEY is sitting at a
table in the crowded visiting room of a
prison. He has tried to make himself as
neat as he can in his prison uniform.
Not knowing who he is, SHELLEY has to
ask one of the supervising PRISON
OFFICERS to point him out. As she
reaches the table, STANLEY stands
nervously.)

SHELLEY:	Mr Wood? (Shaking hands.) How do you do, it's nice to meet you.
STANLEY:	(Nervous, and tongue-tied.) It's very kind of you to come, Mrs Mitchell.
SHELLEY:	My name's 'Shelley'.
STANLEY:	Oh I'm sorry - Mrs Shelley.
SHELLEY:	(Smiles) No, I mean Shelley Mitchell.
STANLEY:	(Nervously) Oh I'm sorry, I didn't mean to be, you must think I'm terribly stupid I'm - erm, I'm sorry, please won't you, please do - (He indicates the opposite side of the table for her to sit at, and then sits himself. During the conversation that follows he is never able directly to meet her eye.)
SHELLEY:	You've been told who I am, that I'm a Voluntary Associate?
STANLEY:	Oh yes.
SHELLEY:	And you know what an Associate is?
STANLEY:	(Helplessly) No.
SHELLEY:	Something a bit like the old idea of prison visitors - only for when you come out rather than when you're inside. I can come and see you in here from time to time, and we can keep in touch afterwards
STANLEY:	Do I have to - sort of report to you?
SHELLEY:	No nothing like that. In fact you don't have to do anything at all; when you come out if you don't want any more to do with me then that's it. But if you did, I'd try to help you with a job or somewhere to live and things like that.
STANLEY:	Well I have got somewhere to live - it's my own house - well it's more of a sort of shack really, it was my mother's, she left it to me when she died.

SHELLEY:	That's fine then. And a job, how about that?
STANLEY:	The last firm I worked for, before I came inside this time, they did say... but I don't know, it's been a long time, the job's gone I should think.
SHELLEY:	And friends, do you have many friends?
STANLEY:	No well if you spend most of your time in these places you see, you don't... I never really needed friends, I wasn't a great one for... my mother was my best friend, you could say, I didn't want anyone else. (Pause) But she's dead now, I don't know what...
SHELLEY:	Well, perhaps we could try to get to know each other a bit before you come out, should we? I'll write now and again, come and see you - even try and get permission for a day's parole if you'd like that.
STANLEY:	A day's... would they let you?
SHELLEY:	They might.
STANLEY:	That would be very good of them wouldn't it, I wonder if they would... I mean I'd give them my word, I wouldn't try to run away or cause trouble. I - do you really think they might?
SHELLEY:	Well, I can only ask.
STANLEY:	Goodness, that'd never... well what a marvellous thing if you... that's really a surprise, I - I don't know how to put this - I hope you don't mind me asking you, but well I mean are you, do you have a job of some kind?
SHELLEY:	A housewife and a mother now; though I'm not very good at either I'm afraid.
STANLEY:	And - that's all?

SHELLEY: (Laughs) It's enough, believe me! Why, what did you think I did?

STANLEY: Nothing, I - I just wondered that's all.

SHELLEY: I used to be a teacher before I was married.

STANLEY: Oh. (Suddenly) You don't - you don't play the piano do you?

SHELLEY: No, I'm not musical at all. Do you?

STANLEY: Oh no.

(SHELLEY is puzzled by this apparently pointless exchange, but decides not to pursue it. STANLEY seems to have made up his mind about something, and now for the first time manages something approaching a smile.)

A day's parole... that would be wonderful. But only of course if you're sure you're not too busy, I mean I wouldn't want to, if it's going to mean a lot of trouble for you to -

SHELLEY: Leave it with me, and I'll see what I can do, all right?

(End of flash back. SHELLEY is driving her car through the streets on the outskirts of London. She passes a park in which some children are on swings, and there are some sailing boats in a pool.)

(Flash back. SHELLEY's car pulls up outside the prison gate, she gets out and goes to it and rings the bell. She is kept waiting at the wicket gate until STANLEY, wearing a prison issue mackintosh, comes out. Together they get into her car after shaking hands.

In the car as she drives, we see STANLEY's face. This is the first time

83

he has been outside prison for over two
years, and the experience is confusing
and almost over-powering. The noise of
the traffic, the bustle, the activity; all
these things are experiences he has
almost forgotten and at first it is over-
whelming. SHELLEY makes no attempt
to talk and concentrates on her driving.)

STANLEY: (Suddenly aware.) Oh please do forgive
me Mrs Mitchell, I'm being very rude
aren't I, I'm very sorry -

SHELLEY: (Smiles) No really, it's all right.

STANLEY: It's just that it's all so... after two
years you forget what it's like.

SHELLEY: I thought you might like to go somewhere
quiet since it's a nice day. How about a
park or somewhere like that?

STANLEY: Oh that'd be wonderful, a park would be
really nice. It's so kind of you Mrs
Mitchell to do all this, I can't tell you
what it means...

(They walk in Regent's Park. At every
gate-way he steps back to let her go first,
anxious to behave correctly. Being with
a young woman is not an experience he is
accustomed to. But he finds it much
easier than he ever thought he would.
They walk through a formal rose garden,
and cross a bridge. At the end of it
STANLEY stops and turns to her.)

It really is, it's so kind of you Mrs
Mitchell to -

SHELLEY: (Not crossly.) Would you do just one
small thing to please me? Please don't
keep telling me it's very good of me -
from now on, let's just take it as said,
shall we?

(They walk on for a while; again they stop. This time they sit on a bench under some trees. STANLEY looks at the grass, at the flowers, at the trees and at the sky.)

STANLEY: I never imagined anything like this. I prayed last night, I said a prayer everything would be all right, that it'd work out. Prayers do get answered sometimes, don't they?

SHELLEY: I thought you might like some tea before you have to go back. I've made a few buns and things, will that be all right?

STANLEY: (The implication doesn't sink in at first.) You mean - you mean have tea at your - ?

SHELLEY: (Nods) That's if you'd like to come, will you?

STANLEY: But Mrs Mitchell, are you sure, I mean you've done so much for me already, I don't know what to say to thank you for -

SHELLEY: What about the promise? (She smiles at him, and STANLEY nods and manages to smile back. They get up and walk away.)

(SHELLEY and STANLEY are just finishing afternoon tea in the sitting room at her house. STANLEY is on his very best behaviour: if he drops a crumb, he brushes it meticulously into his hand and puts it back on his plate. SHELLEY naturally is at ease in her own home. Things she has been showing him are scattered about: magazines, books, photograph albums. STANLEY puts down his cup and saucer on the table.)

STANLEY: I can't remember when I ever ate so much before. It was lovely Mrs Mitchell, it's so good of you to - (He looks at her, and smiles before the reproof is given.)

SHELLEY:	Can't you eat anything more, why don't you try one of these?
STANLEY:	I couldn't possibly, honestly. They're delicious. You know, they're almost exactly the same as my mother used to make. It's all very strange. I've been thinking of it all day.
SHELLEY:	Of what?
STANLEY:	I've got some photographs of her when she was young, about the same age as you. You might almost... there've been moments today, it sounds silly... are you sure you don't play the piano?
SHELLEY:	(Laughs) Quite sure.
STANLEY:	She did, she was a lovely pianist, she used to play and sing for hours. A lovely person, you would have liked her, and I know she'd have liked you.
SHELLEY:	How long ago did she die?
STANLEY:	Nine, nearly ten years. But it still seems like only yesterday. They say you get over things in time... every week it's the same, on the Saturday we always used to go to the pictures, we never missed. Saturday's the worst night, the really lonely one. (Brightening) I can remember her once, you know -
	(MARK, back from school, comes in through the door.)
MARK:	Hello Mummy. (To STANLEY.) Hello.
SHELLEY:	Hello darling. Mark this is Mr Wood - Mr Wood, Mark.
MARK:	(Going over to shake hands.) How do you do Mr Wood?
	(ROBERT rushes in, also back from school. He is covered from head to foot with mud.)

86

SHELLEY:	Robert! What on earth have you been doing?
ROBERT:	I was the goalie, we only lost six four, honest I made some super saves.
SHELLEY:	Well you go and take those filthy things off this minute. All of them - by the back door.
ROBERT:	Can I have one of those buns first?
SHELLEY:	Not until you've washed and tidied yourself up - now go on!
MARK:	Can you play football, Mr Wood, will you have a game with us?
STANLEY:	I'm afraid I'm a bit old for football now. I can do some card tricks though, I used to be able to, shall I show you some?
MARK:	Ooh yes please!
SHELLEY:	I'll go and put their tea on the kitchen table. (She goes out.)

(MARK has brought a pack of playing cards from a drawer and hands them to STANLEY. STANLEY is much more at ease now.)

STANLEY: (With the cards.) I wonder if you've seen this one? Now - four cards across there, face upwards, like that; and now another row of four: and another one, and another one.

(ROBERT has come back into the room. He has taken off his muddy clothes and is wearing his vest and underpants. He goes round the back of STANLEY, and leans over to watch what he is showing MARK; after a few moments he moves round and sits by STANLEY's side.)

Now then this is very difficult. Choose

STANLEY: (Cont)	one of those but don't tell me which one it is. Right? Which line is it in?
MARK:	(Pointing) That one.
STANLEY:	Right. Now we pick them all up, shuffle them, lay them out again face upwards in four rows like this - there we are, that's it. Now then, which line is it in?
MARK:	That one.
STANLEY:	This is the really difficult part. I pick them all up, shuffle them, and divide them into four piles and put them like that face downwards. Point to any pile. That one? Right. Now, you put the four cards in that pile in a row face down. Take any two away. Now take one away of those that's left. Right - now turn up the one that's there - and is that the one you chose?
MARK:	Blimey, how do you do that?
ROBERT:	(Clutching STANLEY's arm.) Me, do it for me now!
	(SHELLEY comes out of the kitchen to tell them their tea is laid. At the door-way she stops.)
SHELLEY:	(Involuntarily) Robert!
	(STANLEY looks up and sees SHELLEY in the door-way watching what is going on. Although she tries hard to conceal it he can read the expression on her face.)
STANLEY:	(Quietly, to ROBERT.) No more card tricks now son - do what your Mum says, there's a good lad. I'll show you some more after you've had your tea.
	(In SHELLEY's car later they are driving back to the prison. STANLEY is looking

out of the window. When they reach the gates, SHELLEY halts the car.)

SHELLEY: We're in good time: it's only quarter past five. Let's have a cigarette before you go in.

(STANLEY takes one, she lights it for him, and then her own. They sit.)

STANLEY: (Quietly) You know, don't you? (SHELLEY nods, exhales: she does not look at him.) When you looked at me when... Mrs Mitchell, I do want you to know, your boys, perhaps you won't believe it but I never, you see people find it so hard to... I love children, I'd never dream of... sometimes I think if I'd only been married and had children of my own... I just can't understand what it is comes over me, I don't think what I'm doing and then afterwards I'm so ashamed... (With great courage he turns his head slowly and looks at her: with great courage too, she looks back. There is nothing reproving in her glance She just wishes she could understand.) Mrs Mitchell, do you think, for someone like me it's... I mean, is it too late or could there be some kind of treatment? Could I be treated... do you think I could?

SHELLEY: Yes, Stanley. Yes I'm sure you could.

(End of flash back. In her car SHELLEY pulls up in the lane outside STANLEY's dilapidated, isolated shack-bungalow. It has a rough patch of untended garden round it. It is of the prefabricated, holiday bungalow type and is at the end of a line of others of a similar kind.

SHELLEY gets out of her car, pushes open the wooden gate, makes her way up

the path and bangs on the front door. No
reply. She hovers uncertainly, unable
to see through the single casement
window, lace curtained at the front. She
walks back down the path, turns for a
final look, and her eye catches sight of
the rear wheel of a bicycle sticking out
at the back of the bungalow. She goes
round to look at it, then comes back and
in doing so passes the casement window
in the side of the house. The lower sash
has been pushed up and the slight wind is
stirring the lace curtains. On tip-toe
she can just see through into the room.
Everything is dark but there is a shadowy
figure in the corner.)

SHELLEY: Stanley? Is that you Stanley?

                (The figure comes into view: it is
                'SPIDER' WEBB. He addresses her in
                the same tones as he uses to the police -
                flat, cautious, non-commital.)

SPIDER: 'E's not 'ere.

SHELLEY: (Politely) Have you any idea what time
                he'll be back?

SPIDER: No, no idea.

SHELLEY: Can you tell me where I could find him?

SPIDER: No. Waitin' for 'im meself.

SHELLEY: When he does come back, would you
                mind telling him Mrs Mitchell called?

SPIDER: Yeh. Yeh I'll do that.

                (Uneasy and disconcerted, SHELLEY
                makes her way to the front of the
                bungalow and starts to go back down the
                path. But it has now struck 'SPIDER'
                that she might be a probation officer or
                someone to do with the law. He jerks

open the front door and goes after her.
He attempts a jovial smile.)

SPIDER: I say - missus! I climbed through the window like, 'cause that's what I always do, see, 'e told me anytime 'e wasn't 'ere just 'op in through the window an' sit down and wait. (While he is saying this he realises he is holding an envelope in his hand. He doesn't want to draw her attention to it and tries to slip it into his pocket. A total failure and he laughs nervously when she notices it. He tries the first unconvincing bluff that comes into his head.) Was goin' to leave a note for 'im, but there's not much point really, I won't bother.

SHELLEY: (Suspiciously) Are you a friend of his?

SPIDER: Oh yes, yeh. Well, kind of yes and no, if you know what I mean, more like sort of.

SHELLEY: Have you seen him in the last few days?

SPIDER: No, no I 'aven't. He hasn't been around a bit. As a matter of fact I was thinkin' it was time I ought to be goin' just when you come. Well, so long then - sorry I can't 'elp yer.

(With affected nonchalance, 'SPIDER' does his best at a friendly smile, saunters round to get his bike, gets on it and peddles off. SHELLEY, uneasily, watches him go. She goes back to her car and drives away.

She stops outside a pub, goes in to look for STANLEY, comes out. She stands hesitantly by her car, then decides she will go back to his bungalow for another look to see if he is there.

SHELLEY's car is driving down the lane
again. A police car is now parked in
front of the bungalow. SHELLEY stops
her car, jumps out, goes to the front
door and goes in. She stops, aghast:
the place is in a tip. Two burly CID men
are there, GARFIELD and WORTLEY,
and they are methodically pulling the
place apart.)

SHELLEY: What do you think you're doing, who are
             you, what do you want?

GARFIELD: (With quiet menace.) We're Police
             Officers madam, with a search warrant,
             carrying out our duty.

SHELLEY: Police? But where's Mr Wood, what's
             happening, what right have you -

GARFIELD: Are you a relative of his madam?

SHELLEY: A relative, no, I'm a friend. Please tell
             me what's going on.

             (WORTLEY brushes past her perfunctorily
             as he gets on with his searching.)

GARFIELD: I can't give you any information, I'm
             sorry.

SHELLEY: You say you're policemen but anyone
             could say that, anyone could.

             (WORTLEY takes his wallet out of his
             pocket, opens it and holds it in front of
             her face so that she can see his
             identification.)

GARFIELD: We're very busy and there's a lot to do,
             so if you wouldn't mind -

SHELLEY: But I'm trying to find out where he is.

GARFIELD: No doubt he'll communicate with you
             himself in time if he wishes to.

SHELLEY:	What's happened to him, please tell me?
GARFIELD:	I can't say madam. I must ask you to leave.
SHELLEY:	But at least tell me where he is.
GARFIELD:	I've no idea. I can only say he's in custody that's all - and I shouldn't really go as far as that.
SHELLEY:	In custody? But where? Why? On what charge?
GARFIELD:	(Heavily) I've been very patient with you, madam, as I'm sure my colleague will agree. The man will be appearing in court tomorrow morning before the local magistrate. And now if you wouldn't mind, we've a lot to do so I'll bid you good day.
	(SHELLEY goes to the door; then she makes one last attempt but before she can speak GARFIELD interrupts her.)
	Ten o'clock the court starts madam; the one half way down the High Street, opposite the cinema. (He gives a smile that flashes on then immediately off.)
	(In her kitchen, JOHN is not even trying to smile at SHELLEY. He is in a towering rage.)
JOHN:	Well where the hell have you been?
SHELLEY:	I'm terribly sorry John, I'd no idea it was so -
JOHN:	Sorry! Good God, do you know you're three hours late? The kids have driven me mad, Mark kicked a football through the back window, Robert's gone off hours ago I've no idea where, Peter was livid I cancelled the golf, I burned the meat to a cinder, the potatoes have boiled to a pulp and -

SHELLEY: John, I'm sorry, what else can I -

JOHN: And I've been trying to do some vitally important sales figures and mucked the whole lot up because I couldn't get five minutes uninterrupted peace and quiet.

SHELLEY: Well leave everything to me now, I'll get on as fast as I can and have the dinner ready as soon as -

JOHN: There won't be any dinner! I told you, the meat's burned.

SHELLEY: All right - we'll open a tin or something.

JOHN: If you think I'm going to have corned beef and potato sludge for Sunday dinner you're mistaken.

SHELLEY: John, Stanley's in trouble, I've had a terrible -

JOHN: Damn Stanley - and damn all your other prisoners too! I'm fed up to the back teeth with the way you put them first all the time! (He picks up his golf clubs.) I'm going to the club for a couple of drinks and a sandwich, then I'm going to have a bloody game of golf with someone - anyone. Oh, and your mother had to get a taxi to catch her train. (As he goes.) Don't keep any corned beef for me. (He slams out of the door. Outside, the car starts up and drives away.)

(MARK comes into the kitchen.)

MARK: Mummy, where on earth have you been?

SHELLEY: I'm sorry, Mark.

MARK: I'm not half hungry. (Pause) Mummy, you're not crying, are you?

SHELLEY: (With her back to him at the sink.) No dear, of course not.

(SHELLEY is in bed; JOHN is just gettin
in.)

SHELLEY: John, I'm sorry. I hate us going to bed
             ... please let's make it up.

JOHN: (Getting into bed and pulling the bed
             clothes up.) I'm very tired, do you mind

             (The following morning, walking along th
             street, SHELLEY is passing the play-
             ground of a large co-educational secondar
             modern school. A casual glance through
             the railings: she walks on, stops, then
             looks back. She's sure she's seen him
             before, though 'SPIDER' looks younger in
             school uniform. He is in goal against the
             wall at one end of the play-ground playing
             football with other boys. A small group
             of girl admirers is watching him. He
             catches sight of SHELLEY looking throug'
             the railings: recognises her, but affects
             not to and turns away to chat up the girls.
             Uneasily, SHELLEY walks on, in time
             coming to the magistrate's court building,
             and goes in.)

             (Inside the lobby at the front, she
             enquires from a uniformed attendant
             POLICEMAN which court STANLEY will
             be appearing in, and goes over in the
             direction he indicates.)

SHELLEY: (To another attendant POLICEMAN.)
             Excuse me, I wonder if you could help
             me? I'm trying to find which court some-
             one will be appearing in. His name's
             Wood, Stanley Wood.

             (Passing, a burly middle-aged man in
             sports jacket and flannels, smoking a
             pipe, stops when he hears the name.
             PHILLIP BREAM, a probation officer.)

BREAM: You've missed him I'm afraid, he was on about half an hour ago in court number one. Are you a relative of his?

SHELLEY: (Disappointed) No, just a friend.

(BREAM didn't know STANLEY had any friends: he looks at her curiously.)

BREAM: The police asked for a remand in custody, it was over in two minutes. Have you known him long? (SHELLEY shakes her head.) You must have met him while he was in prison then?

SHELLEY: Yes. I'm a Voluntary Associate.

BREAM: (No expression.) Got a few minutes for a chat? (SHELLEY nods.) Let's go in my office, it's just there. I'm a Probation Officer, my name's Phillip Bream.

SHELLEY: I'm Mrs Shelley Mitchell.

(They come into BREAM's office from the corridor: he indicates a chair for her to sit in, opposite his at the other side of the desk.)

BREAM: Is he the first prisoner you've associated with?

SHELLEY: Oh no, I've been an associate about four years now.

BREAM: (No expression.) Some probation officers aren't all that keen on voluntary associates. They think they're amateur do-gooders.

SHELLEY: (Levelly) Yes I know.

BREAM: (Equally levelly, not ingratiating.) Don't see it that way myself. (He lights his pipe.) If after-care's ever going to be anything better than the shambles it is, there's plenty of scope - and need - for

BREAM: (Cont)	both amateurs and professionals. Stanley Wood... he's a problem, isn't he?
SHELLEY:	You know him then?
BREAM:	He was on licence to me before he came out at the end of his previous sentence. 'Fraid I never got anywhere.
SHELLEY:	I don't seem to have either. What's he charged with?
BREAM:	Usual thing. There's only one charge so far. It's purely a holding one, the police'll use the time he's in custody to make further enquiries. Suppose by the time they've finished they'll end up with seven or eight charges as usual.
SHELLEY:	And then?
BREAM:	In view of his previous record the magistrate'll hand him on to the assizes so he can get another good long stretch of imprisonment.
SHELLEY:	My God, and he was trying so hard -
BREAM:	If only he'd make some attempt to get treatment, try and find a way out of this perpetual -
SHELLEY:	But he did.
BREAM:	(Astonished) Did he? I haven't heard about it, tell me about it, what happened?
SHELLEY:	He asked me if I thought it was too late, and I said no it wasn't. But wanting treatment and getting it aren't quite the same thing are they? (Flash back. By the side of a river, SHELLEY and STANLEY are walking. He is out with her for another day's parole. STANLEY is looking at the water and the boats which are pulled up along the shore.)

STANLEY: I never thought of the river you know, that was a lovely idea to come here. It's good of them at the prison to let me come out a few times like this with you, they're not all bad people in those places. The governor, Mr Lincoln, he's a nice man you know, the sort of person you could really talk to if you ever had a proper chance. But there's so many isn't there, so many prisoners, it's all the staff can do just to remember people's names most of the time. (Pause) I'm not a great one for mixing with other people, more of a solitary man... a bit like my father, I suppose. He was a sailor you know, often we didn't see him almost from one year's end to the next. My mother was very unhappy with him, she never said much but I knew she was, when he was home there were always terrible rows. Terrible rows... I was only a kid, but if I saw her crying I'd set on him, I would, I'd pummel him with my fists. Eight or nine, that's all I'd be, but I'd really go for him I would. I couldn't bear ever to see her cry. (Pause) Then one day he just didn't come back any more.

SHELLEY: Did she ever think of marrying again?

STANLEY: Oh no, she didn't believe in that sort of thing. She always used to say she didn't need anyone else, as long as she'd got me. Devoted she was, devoted herself to me. She was... well she was like a wife to me really she was, can you understand, only better than a wife in fact, because I'd known her all my life, hadn't I, and you can't get any closer can you to anyone than that. Real pals we were, neither of us wanted anyone else at all. And she always understood me, always kind... even when I started getting into trouble, she always forgave me, you know. She said she was

STANLEY: (Cont)	sure I'd just forgotten myself, we'd both forget about it and start again. If she was alive today I'm sure she'd help me, and tell me what to do.
SHELLEY:	(Puzzled) What to do?
STANLEY:	I'm sure you meant it for the best. Las time you said it wasn't too late. When I got back that day with you, I asked the governor, and he said it was. (Flash back. The prison governor, DAVID LINCOLN, is sitting at his desk. In front of him, SHELLEY is standing, furious.)
SHELLEY:	(Angrily) Did you say that?
LINCOLN:	Yes I did. But -
SHELLEY:	It was you who told me he wouldn't accep treatment! And then when he does come round to the idea -
LINCOLN:	I know it must sound strange to you Mrs Mitchell, but if you'd allow me to explain -
SHELLEY:	Strange? It sounds worse than that, it sounds what it is - monstrous!
LINCOLN:	(Patiently) Yes I agree it must seem like that to you. But I'm afraid there's been a misunderstanding - I did tell him that it was too late, but what I meant, and quite honestly I thought he'd understood, was that it was too late for me to get anything started so near to the end of his sentence. There are nothing like the psychiatric services that are needed inside prison. It takes a long time to arrange, and by the time we'd done it he' be almost due for release.
SHELLEY:	(Angrily) But good God, you've had him for three years, why on earth couldn't something have been begun ages ago?

LINCOLN: (Determined not to be ruffled.) Mrs
Mitchell, I've told you before: treatment
can't be given to someone who refuses to
accept he needs it. I've over a thousand
men in this prison, and Heaven knows
it's difficult enough to help those who
want to be helped. Don't imagine we just
like keeping people in, full stop, with
nothing happening to them at all. It costs
over twenty pounds a week to keep one
man in prison. I could think of a dozen
better ways we could spend the money - it
must be cheaper in the long run to do
things for people and treat them, rather
than just imprison them. But in Stanley
Wood's case, all I could do as a last hope
for him was put him in touch with you, to
see if you could get anywhere. All right,
you did - but you realise the day his
sentence ends, he goes out. I can't keep
him in here to continue whatever treatment
might have been started. The only thing I
could suggest is that you can persuade him
to have treatment outside.

(SHELLEY and STANLEY are sitting in
the sitting room at SHELLEY's house:
she has brought him there on another
day's parole.)

STANLEY: I'm frightened, three weeks, it's not very
long now is it... you forget, you know, in
prison you feel nothing more can happen
to you, nothing worse. And then one day
it hits you, you're coming out... and you
get afraid. Silly things, I remember the
last time I came out all the 'phone boxes
had been changed, you needed different
coins. It takes ages... and the
bungalow'll be in a mess. I've got to find
work... the older you get, the worse it
seems. And now you want me to do this
as well...

SHELLEY: It won't be easy. But I'm sure you can
             get through it, I'm sure you can, some-
             how.

STANLEY: But going to an ordinary doctor, it's not
             like having treatment in prison is it?
             'Yes', he'll say, 'and what's the matter
             with you?' It's not like a pain in the
             tummy or a sore throat, is it? I mean
             how do you start telling him, what's he
             going to think of me?

SHELLEY: If he's a good doctor, he'll send you on
             to a hospital, to a specialist. And you
             musn't think you'll be the first one he's
             ever come across, because I'm certain
             you won't.

STANLEY: Perhaps he'll just regard it as an
             unfortunate illness, do you think? I've
             just got this thing wrong with me... I
             suppose everybody's got something,
             haven't they, some of them even worse.
             And this is what I've got, this is my
             share...

             (SHELLEY in her car is waiting outside
             the gates of a hospital. STANLEY
             comes running out towards her. She
             opens the car door and he gets in:
             thankfully he takes the cigarette she
             offers him. He is smiling.)

             It wasn't too bad after all Shelley, I did
             it, so that's the worst over, isn't it, I
             got there! And they do, they say they do
             think they can help me. Today they just
             took down details and things, I'm to go
             back in three weeks time and they'll
             make a start.

             (End of flash back. SHELLEY now is in
             BREAM's office again.)

BREAM: But it didn't help?

HELLEY: Quarter of an hour's psychotherapy,
            once a month - staff problems, a different
            doctor nearly every. time. It was all a
            case of next time we'll really get down
            to it. . . he had to start again at the
            beginning, explain it all to yet another
            new doctor. No-one ever gave him
            consistent individual attention. If he'd
            been a private patient it'd've been
            different. But of course he didn't
            complain, he didn't demand that they got
            on with it. Just said 'Thank you very
            much, doctor yes I do understand how
            busy you are here, I'll come back next
            month'.

BREAM: And it went on like that?

SHELLEY: Until about six weeks ago; he told me he
            wasn't very happy, he wasn't sure if the
            hospital was doing him much good. Local
            boys kept coming round to his house. I
            wish I knew why to one man it's meaning-
            less, and to another it's a temptation that
            he can't resist. What's the difference in
            the way men are made, how does it
            happen, how much is it really their fault?

BREAM: I don't know. And I don't think people want
            to know: they'd sooner just punish some-
            one, and if psychiatrists can't come up
            with an answer straight off they think
            psychiatry's a waste of time.

SHELLEY: Can it really help? I mean, if it gets a
            chance - with a man like him?

BREAM: Oh yes, I think it can. They haven't got all
            the answers, but they do have some. This
            sort of case I'd have thought was
            comparatively straight forward. Emotional
            retardation, someone who's never
            developed any relationships beyond the
            childhood level. He was kept a child, you
            see, wasn't he, by his mother? Devoted to
            her, and she was to him, and never allowed

BREAM:
(Cont)

him to break away. So what happens?
He's only at ease with children: other
children, because he's still one of them
And what he does with them is exactly
the same as children do with each other
among themselves. Only because
physically he's grown up, everyone's
horrified about it.

SHELLEY:

There must be something I can do. Do
you think I ought to go to court?

BREAM:

Someone ought to... I don't know, some
one ought to say something. The court
granted him legal aid this morning,
should I find out the name of his solicitor
for you?

SHELLEY:

Please. Perhaps I could make a start by
going to see them.

(SHELLEY is sitting opposite a young
solicitor, LAMB, in his office. LAMB
is looking at the cover of an unopened
file.)

LAMB:

A legal aid case, I see we've only had it
a day or two. This is rather difficult for
me Mrs Mitchell, you appreciate
confidentiality doesn't allow me to discuss
a client's affairs with a stranger. I don't
doubt you are, as you say, a friend of his
but I'm sure you'll understand.

SHELLEY:

Of course, I don't want to discuss anything
I've merely come to say one or two things
to you that I hope you could use in his
defence.

LAMB:

(Opens the file and glances at it.) He's
charged with what, now let me see... ah
yes. (He puts the tips of his fingers
together and leans back in his chair and
looks at her.) I can't prevent you telling
me things of course, if there was anything
particular you wanted to say.

SHELLEY: I want to try and help him. (LAMB nods
            professionally. His face indicates
            nothing. SHELLEY struggles on.) I
            believe it's, it's not known how many
            charges there'll be altogether - but
            something can still be said in his defence.

LAMB: Which we of course shall certainly say.

SHELLEY: I'm what is called a Voluntary Associate,
            I was introduced to him while he was in
            prison last time, and the idea is I should
            try to help him when he comes out -

LAMB: Admirable.

SHELLEY: I encouraged him to try and get
            psychiatric treatment. And in fact he
            was still having it when he was arrested.
            (LAMB nods.) Well - I think that should
            be made clear.

LAMB: Yes, we will certainly consider it. But
            that sort of argument you see - well, it
            could boomerang, couldn't it?
            Psychiatric treatment was making no
            difference, do you follow?

SHELLEY: But the amount he was getting was nothing
            like sufficient, that's the whole point.

LAMB: (Politely) Are you medically qualified
            yourself Mrs Mitchell?

SHELLEY: No I'm not, I'm simply concerned to try
            and -

LAMB: Quite so. Well, do rest assured we shall
            do everything we can to see he gets the
            most lenient sentence possible. But after
            all this is by no means his first offence is
            it?

SHELLEY: No but - well what exactly would you hope
            to achieve for him?

LAMB: (Looking down at the contents of the
            folder.) Depending on the number of
            charges, but I should think five years was
            reasonable.

SHELLEY:	Five years? Look - (She realises it's hopeless.) I suppose how many charges the police eventually bring is important then?
LAMB:	Oh yes of course.
SHELLEY:	Well is it necessary to make a separate charge concerning every boy who was present? I mean, perhaps if you spoke to the police -
LAMB:	(A slight smile: then he realises she is quite serious, and that he must get rid o her as quickly and politely as possible.) We're on very good terms with the police, Mrs Mitchell, I've always found them most helpful and co-operative.
SHELLEY:	(Icily) Yes I'm sure you have. (Standin I see... well, thank you for your help.
LAMB:	Not at all. Good afternoon Mrs Mitchell (His smile lasts until she has gone out through the door of his office, then it fades at once. His face indicates that he thinks she must be out of her mind.)

(SHELLEY is going into the police statio and approaching the desk inside the entrance, at which is a POLICE SERGEANT.) |
SHELLEY:	My name is Mrs Mitchell, I wonder if I could talk to someone about a man called Stanley Wood please?
DESK SERGEANT:	(Amiably) Yes certainly you could, madam. Chief Inspector Sands has got somebody with him at the moment, he'll not be long though if you wouldn't mind waiting. I've just made a pot of tea, would you like a cup?
SHELLEY:	(Surprised by this enthusiastic reception. No, no thank you; thank you very much.

DESK SERGEANT: Do sit down over there madam, I'm sure he'll not be more than a few minutes.

(SHELLEY sits on a bench. After a few moments, CHIEF INSPECTOR SANDS comes out with a woman and her small boy, who is MARVIN HURST. He brings them into the lobby and the woman goes out with her arm round MARVIN's shoulder. The boy has been crying. When they have gone, the CHIEF INSPECTOR turns back.

SHELLEY is in his office. CHIEF INSPECTOR SANDS is about to sit at his desk again.)

SANDS: Very sad business, very unpleasant, won't keep you longer than we have to though. (Picking up papers and leafing through them.) Now where are we, Mrs Mitchell did you say, let me see, Mitchell, which one is your little chap then?

SHELLEY: (Firmly) Stanley Wood.

SANDS: Stanley Wood, Stanley... (He looks up sharply.) I beg your pardon?

SHELLEY: Stanley Wood - I'm his friend.

SANDS: (As politely as he can manage.) Are you indeed? Pardon me saying so madam but in that case I think you've come to the wrong place.

SHELLEY: I was told it depended on how many charges you were going to make against -

SANDS: Not at all: it depends on the evidence madam, nothing else.

SHELLEY: But you decide whether to proceed or not.

SANDS: On the contrary, if an offence or offences have been committed, we gather the facts and put them forward: that's all.

SHELLEY:	Though you could overlook something if you wanted to?
SANDS:	A most curious idea of the police you have madam, if I may say so.
SHELLEY:	I've come to ask you if you'll give him a chance.
SANDS:	A chance? That is a decision for the court. I shall do my duty, no more and no less. Madam I don't doubt your intentions are of the best, but this is most improper. Believe me, I've known this man Wood for many years, I don't mind telling you in my personal opinion he's a menace, there's only one place for him and that's -
SHELLEY:	But sending him back to prison over and over again is doing no good.
SANDS:	At least it keeps him out of the way so he can't indulge in his - (He controls himself.) You might see it rather differently if you had children yourself.
SHELLEY:	I have, I've two little boys.
SANDS:	Then all I can say is that it takes all kinds to make a world doesn't it?
SHELLEY:	Haven't you any pity?
SANDS:	I most certainly have - for these unfortunate children and the distress it causes them. No-one ever seems to think about the victims nowadays.
SHELLEY:	But surely you can see there's more to it than -
SANDS:	And if you'll forgive me for saying so I have pity for you too madam, that you should be wasting your time and energy on a pervert like Stanley Wood.
SHELLEY:	(Angrily) He's a human being.
SANDS:	I would say that was a matter of personal opinion madam.

(In his cell on remand before conviction,
STANLEY is sitting on the edge of his
bed and trying to write a letter. After a
time he crumples it up and puts it in his
pocket. He takes out his tobacco tin and
rolls himself a cigarette and lights it.)

(In her kitchen, SHELLEY is sitting at
the table, trying to write a letter. She
is smoking. Her eyes wander round the
room. A few children's toys here and
there, and among them a sailing yacht.)

(STANLEY and SHELLEY are walking
along by the side of a river estuary, past
sailing boats pulled up on the mud. They
are going over some grass dunes towards
a shack in the distance.)

STANLEY: I'm glad you came down Shelley, it was
nice of you, I wanted you to see where I
lived. It's not very smart I'm afraid,
but it suited us, my mother and me we
both liked it. It can be quite pretty in the
summer. I had a boat, not a big one,
something like that one over there, only
a bit smaller. (He looks away from
SHELLEY, and at the boat.) I can't talk
to the doctors at the hospital, they're so
busy... it was just like that one, a bit
smaller, it needed a lot doing to it.
Boys, they'd come and ask if they could
scrub the paint-work for you, help you
push it out into the water. That was how
it began. It was very hot, a Saturday
afternoon, two little boys, they helped
me, they were asking me if I'd take them
out for a ride in it. Very hot... they
decided they'd jump over the side for a
swim. No costumes on, when they got
back in the boat they were running around,
fooling about. I told them to get dressed,
but they didn't, and then... I must admit,

108

STANLEY:
(Cont)

I did, I did lay hands on them. Nothing
serious, don't think that, I didn't attack
them or anything like that. Only playing
about, touching them, that was as far as
it went. They didn't seem to mind, it wa
all like just a harmless bit of fun at the
time. They were jolly and laughing, the
said they'd see me the week after. But
they must have told their parents I
suppose. They didn't come back; the
police did. They took me to court straigh
away for it, I was given six months...
Thirty, I think I was then, or thirty one;
to end up suddenly one day like that, bang
straight off in prison... you don't believe
it could happen to you. My mother
couldn't grasp it at all; and I looked at it
the same way too, it was just something
that happened, no accounting for it really
It'd come on me suddenly, I couldn't
think what had possessed me, I couldn't
even think about it. I was ashamed of my
self, really ashamed... I'm sorry, I
shouldn't have told you that, I'm sorry, I
got carried away.

SHELLEY:

No Stanley: I'm glad you did.

(They are coming into STANLEY's
bungalow.)

STANLEY:

This is it. It was my uncle's originally,
my mother bought it off him cheap. It
used to look much tidier and nicer when
she was alive. She wanted to come back
and die here, they sent her home from
hospital. They couldn't do anything for
her. After she'd gone, being alone, it
was awful, I kept thinking that she was
coming back you know, I tried to forget
about her, I started to drink, I just used
to sit here on my own missing her and
drinking cheap wine. All the kids knew,
I was notorious in the district, any time

STANLEY:
(Cont)

they wanted a bit of money to spend on
sweets they'd come along. Sometimes
I'd find notes pushed under the door
saying they were coming... I can't get
away from that, I did, when I saw the
note I did get a thrill from it, knowing
they were coming to see me. It couldn't
be allowed to go on, could it? Once the
police came in and actually found it going
on, these boys running about half
dressed and me sitting over there on the
bed drunk. Oh I'm sorry, would you
like a cup of tea? (He does what he can
to clear old newspapers off a chair to
make a place for her to sit down on. He
goes to the stove and puts a kettle on.)
The judge was the same one as I'd had in
the previous case. He remembered me
all right, he said 'You're a menace, you
are, I'm going to put a stop to your
activities once and for all', so he gave
me eight years. Eight years... I really
did, I thought I might as well be dead.
I'd sit in my cell and think 'What's the
use, this is the finish, it's all over now,
this is where I shall spend the rest of my
days'. The only thing I was thankful for
was my mother hadn't lived to see where
I'd ended up, that would have killed her
even if the illness hadn't. Other people,
you can't expect them to understand
about it, can you? They say 'Well I don't
feel like that, so how can he?' They
think it's disgusting, it's horrible... it's
only natural people should think indecent
assault means much more than it says.
They think it must mean trying to, well
you know an actual sexual act, they
think you must be dirty and horrible and
cruel... it's like a sort of illness that
comes on you, you've got it, and you can't
think what to do...

(SHELLEY is still sitting in her kitchen trying to write her letter. JOHN comes in, just back from work. He seems strangely elated.)

JOHN: (Quietly, because of the row they had.) Hello darling, sorry I'm late.

SHELLEY: That's all right, I'd no idea what the time was, I'm afraid I haven't even started to get your -

(JOHN comes over to her, puts his arms round her and kisses her.)

JOHN: We're not going to bother about supper tonight! We're going out. We'll have a drink first, then we'll go to that little Italian restaurant that -

SHELLEY: I've got some food in, it won't take me long to -

JOHN: It can keep till tomorrow. Come on, I'm going to pour you a large drink. (He goes off to the sitting room.) Had a good day? (He brings a drink back for her, and is carrying another for himself.)

SHELLEY: No, not really. (She catches sight of herself in the mirror.) God, I look a sight.

JOHN: (Kissing her on the back of the neck.) You look beautiful to me. Here. (He hands her the drink.)

SHELLEY: John, the world's so full of -

JOHN: The world's full of all sorts of things, some bad and some good. I'll tell you a good one - I'm going to be made North West Area Sales Manager!

SHELLEY: John! Really? Oh that's marvellous, I'm so glad!

JOHN: (Holding up his glass.) So - a little

JOHN:
(Cont)
celebration! (He drinks.) A thousand a year more, help with buying a house, more expenses, a larger car -

SHELLEY:
Buying a house?

JOHN:
Well, we'll have to live up there, Liverpool, Manchester, I'm told the outskirts are quite nice, someone was saying there were some nice places in Cheshire if you start looking round, you can very easily -

SHELLEY:
I can't take it in yet, it's so sudden. When will we be moving?

JOHN:
Oh, three or four months. They want me to go up for a week and meet the office people there, get things sorted out. You can come with me. Your mother'll come over and look after the kids. The sooner we start looking at houses the better.

SHELLEY:
The end of this month. (JOHN nods.) That's quite soon isn't it?

JOHN:
Well we've got to get on with things, and the sooner -

SHELLEY:
It's just that I'm a bit confused, Stanley's coming up for trial at the assizes in a week or two, I feel I ought to be there. John, I know you think it's ridiculous -

JOHN:
(Smiles) Look, let's not talk about it for tonight eh? We'll go out and have our meal and celebrate. (Cheerfully) Are the boys in bed yet?

SHELLEY:
No, they're still in the bath.

JOHN:
I'll go up and tell them they can stay up until we come back.

(JOHN goes. After a moment SHELLEY follows. She stands at the bathroom door: JOHN is expansive and ebullient,

and fools about with MARK and
ROBERT, lifting them out of the bath
and wrapping them up in towels. The
normal heterosexual man, unthinking
about and unafraid of physical contact
with two small undressed boys. As
SHELLEY stands there she hears
STANLEY's voice.)

STANLEY: (Voice over.) I love children... sometimes I think if I'd married and had
some of my own... I don't understand.

(SHELLEY is visiting STANLEY while
he is in prison on remand. This is a
closed visit in a visiting-box: a narrow
cubicle, one of a row, each divided
across the centre with a window of wired
glass between the prisoner and the
visitor. A strip of perforated zinc round
the edge of the glass so that conversation
can be made: but it is not easy, since in
all the other boxes prisoners and visitors
are trying to talk to each other too, and
the noise and hubbub is constant.
STANLEY is in refracted vision. Sometimes he is clearly seen, sometimes as
he moves his image blurs. It is almost
impossible for SHELLEY to hear everything he says. His head is lowered and
he is embarrassed; but there is more to
it than this. He is inside and she is out,
and already he has accepted that this is
where he'll stay; already mentally he is
three quarters a prisoner again. To
himself he is guilty, convicted, sentenced
and imprisoned.)

... Difficult, you see... I mean, a lot of
work they have to... the best they can
I'm sure... very good of them to bother,
really...

SHELLEY: (Desperately) Stanley, I can't hear you
properly.

STANLEY: (Nods) You never can hear properly in
               these visiting-boxes, it's always like
               this, you'd think they'd try and do some-
               thing about it wouldn't you... (He looks
               round vaguely at his situation.)

SHELLEY: Can you speak up a bit, what were you
               just saying?

STANLEY: ... an awful lot to do... I'm very grate-
               ful to them... the solicitors.

SHELLEY: To the solicitors?

STANLEY: (Nods) If you'd tell them for me how
               much I appreciate it...

SHELLEY: Stanley - look - what I'm trying to say to
               you is that I want us to make a fight of it.
               (STANLEY nods, though it hardly seems
               to be relevant to him personally.) I want
               to make a fight of it for you! To try to
               get you out - to go on from here - to try
               and start again -

STANLEY: (Nods placidly.) Well yes I should think
               I'll get about five, wouldn't you? There'll
               be a third off for good behaviour, so
               that'll only be just over three years. So
               then I suppose we could -

SHELLEY: (Desperately) No Stanley, I mean instead
               of - instead of your going back to prison,
               not after you come out again, do you
               understand?

STANLEY: (Nods) Oh yes. (Still in his own world.)
               I shall plead guilty - I think they've
               settled on six charges altogether now.
               I'll plead guilty - that might help them to
               be lenient a bit. (He looks straight at
               her.) I am guilty.

SHELLEY: Yes Stanley, I know you are, but I want
               you to fight - can you hear what I'm
               saying? Please will you listen carefully?
               (STANLEY nods.) I don't think you ought
               to go back to prison at all. I want to try
               and get the court to -

STANLEY: It's awfully noisy, isn't it, I'm very sorry Mrs Mitchell that you should have to be in a place like this, they ought to do a bit better really shouldn't they?

SHELLEY: (Still trying to get through.) I want to try and get you properly represented. I'm going to see if I can -

STANLEY: Yes well I'm very grateful to you Mrs Mitchell, I really am, really, I'm very grateful, please don't think I'll ever forget all you've tried to do for me... (He seems to be, and is, moving backwards. SHELLEY is losing sight of him and contact with him.)

(In the sitting room of her home, SHELLEY is having tea with her mother MRS LEE.)

MRS LEE: You're looking very depressed dear. I really can't understand it, I should have thought you'd be very excited about it all, the new job and looking for a house and a new start up in the -

SHELLEY: Oh I'll feel better once I get up there, I suppose. It's just that I'm worried about the trial, that's all.

MRS LEE: Trial dear, what trial?

SHELLEY: Just a man.

MRS LEE: You know, I've never been able to understand how you could get so involved with prisoners, Shelley, I just can't make it out. I mean, there are so many other worth-while things - orphaned children, famine relief -

SHELLEY: Suitable subjects for charity you mean? Prisoners are human like anyone else, you know.

MRS LEE: Yes but it always seems to make you so

MRS LEE: Cont)	depressed. You've got a good home, a wonderful husband, nice children - what more do you want out of life? Aren't you happy?
SHELLEY:	Oh yes, I'm happy. But being happy isn't just patting yourself on the back and thinking how lucky you are. Being happy makes you more conscious of what other people haven't got. Being thankful for what you have doesn't mean not caring if others haven't got the same.
MRS LEE:	Yes dear, but why prisoners? I mean it's not as if - well, we don't go round robbing people, hitting them on the head, shooting policemen and -
SHELLEY:	No, nor do most of the men in prison. In fact what they do, the majority of them, it's unbelievable they should be there, for such trivial, pathetic, inept -
MRS LEE:	Well this man for instance that you're so concerned about now, what does he do?
SHELLEY:	(Levelly) Indecent assault on little boys.
MRS LEE:	Shelley, I do wish you wouldn't say things just to try and shock me.
SHELLEY:	I'm not, it's true.
MRS LEE:	(Incredulously) Indecent assault on little boys? Shelley, you're not -
SHELLEY:	It does happen mother. You can't bury your head in the sand.
MRS LEE:	Shelley you must be... I'm a reasonably broad-minded person, but if there's one thing I simply can't stand it's things like that.
SHELLEY:	Things like what?
MRS LEE:	Hurting children, perversions of the most horrible -
SHELLEY:	I don't think he does hurt them. I'm not

SHELLEY: (Cont)	even sure it's worth even calling it a perversion.
MRS LEE:	I simply don't wish to hear any more about it if you don't -
SHELLEY:	That's the trouble; people would much sooner rely on their own prejudices. (Pause) Shall I tell you exactly what he does?
MRS LEE:	No thank you!
SHELLEY:	Well I'm going to - because I think you should know what somebody so far has spent nearly twenty years of his life in prison for. 'Indecent assault' - the imagination runs riot doesn't it? Well all it means is he fondles small boys - their legs, their bottoms, their genitals
MRS LEE:	(Outraged) Shelley!
SHELLEY:	He's not a sex maniac, he doesn't try and rape them, he doesn't use force against them - that would be buggery. All he does is just touch them, that's all And he doesn't go out looking for them either: they come to him. They don't mind, most of them; they know what he is and what he does, and they go and put themselves in a position where - though of course you can't expect people to swallow that. And when it comes out, everyone throws up their hands in horror Not at the children because they're dear sweet little innocent things - but at this monster in their midst. Whether what he does actually harms them or not is open to argument; most little boys play about with each other, I've got two of my own, so I do know a bit about what I'm talking about - and they don't all necessarily grow up into raging homo- sexuals just because of that.
MRS LEE:	Shelley I won't listen to any more, I've never heard such filthy disgusting -

117

SHELLEY: (Raging) All right, don't listen, pretend it doesn't happen! Only when you've calmed down try and think about it, think about what can happen. How a wretched sad man whose mother held him into an emotional vice so he couldn't ever have a grown-up relationship is doing a life sentence because of it - a life sentence on instalments. All because people like you won't think about what he actually does or how to help him. All they can think of is punishment. He even tried to get treatment this time, and he failed - or we failed him, perhaps it would be truer to say. The police think they're engaged in the fight against crime every time they catch him. And next week he'll come up in court for sentence, and the solicitor he's been given on legal aid will be satisfied if he gets anything less than five years.

MRS LEE: (Quietly) I'm sorry Shelley, I'm too old. To my way of thinking, unfortunate though it all no doubt is, we can well do without people like that.

(In the school playground 'SPIDER' is throwing a football about with some of his friends.)

DANNY: Eh Spider, you see in the paper that old man Wood's bin sent to assizes? What's that mean?

SPIDER: That's the big court - the top one - judges and all that.

GORDON: My old man says he'll be put away now good and proper. Serve 'im right.

DANNY: Well you've 'ad your quid now Spider, ain't you?

GORDON: Quid - what quid?

DANNY:	Old Spider wrote 'im a letter, didn't you? Asked 'im for a quid, said 'e could introduce 'im to some boys.
SPIDER:	Give over. I never.
DANNY:	You did, I saw it, you showed it me.
SPIDER:	I was only 'avin' you on, it was a joke, I never sent it.
MICHAEL:	I liked old Stanley, I thought he was nice
DANNY:	'E was a dirty old man.

(In their living room late in the evening, JOHN and SHELLEY having got the children to bed, are sitting down and having coffee. JOHN is looking at manufacturer's leaflets about motor-cars.)

JOHN:	Peter's brother's got one of those, he says it's fantastic, forty-eight to the gallon or something like that. Anyway, as it's going to be your car, the choice is up to you - what do you fancy?

(SHELLEY is trying hard to be interested but isn't. She glances at the leaflet JOHN has handed her, stubs out her cigarette.)

SHELLEY:	John do you really think we need two cars? I mean after all, we've managed so far with one all right, it's not been -
JOHN:	We don't need two no, it'd just be much more convenient for you that's all. Give you more independence, help you get around. (Laughs) I don't understand, I'd have thought you'd have been delighted with the idea of having a car of your own.
SHELLEY:	Yes of course I shall John, you know that Only I... well, I was wondering if we could use the money for something else, that's all. It'll cost what, six or seven hundred?

JOHN: We can afford it easily now. Houses up in the north are much cheaper and -

SHELLEY: I've been making enquiries about something else, I'm told it would cost about two hundred pounds.

JOHN: (Smiles) Well if you'd sooner have something else - what is it?

SHELLEY: Get a man legally represented, with the best solicitor and barrister I could find; privately, not on legal aid.

(The smile fades from JOHN's face. He puts down his coffee cup and goes and sits by SHELLEY on the settee. He puts his arm round her shoulder.)

JOHN: (Quietly) In all my life Shelley I've never loved anyone as much as I love you. And I've never loved you as much as I love you now. (Very quietly.) But you can't Shelley. We can't. There's a line, love ... and this is it.

(They look at each other. After a moment SHELLEY does her best to smile; she nods.)

(In his prison cell, the convicted STANLEY sits on the edge of his bed. He rolls a cigarette, lights it, stares. There is no emotion at all on his face. In a way, since he had never expected anything else, about all he can feel now is a certain amount of relief that it is over.)

(It is morning assembly time in the school. In the hall the pupils - 'SPIDER', MICHAEL, GORDON, ALAN, STEPHEN and MARVIN - are dotted about here and there. 'SPIDER' as usual is fooling about with some of the girls. To the

accompaniment of the piano the school
children are singing, not very tunefully,
one of the regular school assembly
songs.)

PUPILS:

(Singing)
'Bring me my bow of burning gold!
Bring me my arrow of desire!
Bring me my spear! Oh clouds unfold!
Bring me my chariot of fire!
I shall not cease from mortal strife,
Nor shall my sword sleep in my hand,
Till we have built Jerusalem
In England's green and pleasant land...'

(The prisoners are exercising in the
prison yard. STANLEY is walking on
his own, apart from the rest. The
singing of 'Jerusalem' continues over.

The end captions roll up over the view of
the exercise yard and the sound of the
singing. Then:-

It could happen, and it did - exactly like
this. His name is not 'Stanley Wood':
but, like him, he is in prison again.
This time he is serving a sentence of six
years.)

FINISH

When the Bough Breaks

For Joan Court

WHEN THE BOUGH BREAKS

This play illustrates the fine work carried out by the
NSPCC and ancillary social services. When Sheila
Gosse's baby is found to have serious and unexplained
injuries suspicion falls on her powerfully-built
husband. But somehow the jigsaw doesn't quite fit
together and Margaret Ashdown, the young social
worker, is determined to find out why.

WHEN THE BOUGH BREAKS was first shown on BBC-1 in May 1971, and repeated in 1972.

Sheila Gosse .... CHERYL KENNEDY

Eddie Gosse .... NEIL McCARTHY

Margaret Ashdown .... HANNAH GORDON

Audrey Campbell ..... EDITH MACARTHUR

It was produced by Irene Shubik and directed by James Ferman.

CAST

SHEILA GOSSE, aged 21

MARGARET ASHDOWN, 28

GEORGE STANDISH, early 30s

SISTER POTTS, middle-aged

RECEPTIONIST

NURSE

SISTER THOMPSON, aged 50

DR DHONDI, a Pakistani,
                casualty doctor

DR JOHN CUNNINGHAM,
                Consultant Paediatrician

MISS HAMILTON

EDDIE GOSSE

MR FOST

TIMMY, aged 4

AUDREY CAMPBELL

PDSA MAN

Ambulance Attendants, Baby, Patients.

A white Mini-Minor is bumping along a rough cart track
which crosses a field of long grass. The field belongs to a
farm on the outskirts of a small town. It is at the back of
the farm, and at the end of it on a worn patch of ground
stand three caravans. This is not a holiday area and these
are not holiday caravans: it's cheap accommodation for
transients, rent payable weekly in advance. One has been
unoccupied for some time: by the other two are screened-
off chemical toilets and dustbins overflowing with refuse.
When the sun shines, living here you could almost imagine
you were in the country: when it's raining, it's difficult to
escape the fact that you're only a step away from home-
lessness.

As the Mini-Minor reaches these caravans a young girl,
unconscious, is being loaded into an ambulance on a
stretcher. She is SHEILA GOSSE, 21, with long golden hair
and cornflower-blue eyes. Her face is chalk-white and
immobile. Even when it is not, the porcelain doll childish-
ness of it soon loses its impact of prettiness, because her
face is always expressionless and characterless. Wrapped
in blankets on the stretcher she is being lifted into the
ambulance by its ATTENDANTS. They close the doors, and
the ambulance moves off.

Just too late to stop it, MARGARET ASHDOWN, 28, a small
neat girl in a two-piece suit, gets out of the Mini-Minor.
She hesitates, watches the ambulance disappear across the
field back towards the lane. Behind her the wintry wind
bustles through the trees. Against them comes up the title:-

WHEN THE BOUGH BREAKS

MARGARET goes towards the end caravan. Watching her
from the steps of the next one to it is GEORGE STANDISH,
small and balding, in his early thirties, with a thin face
and a colourless shirt.

STANDISH: (Calling) No good, no-one there.

MARGARET: (Anxious, but calm.) What's happened?

STANDISH:	(Coming down the steps of his caravan.) You from the press? It was me found her, my name's Standish, George Standish, I'm their neighbour. Terrible shock, lovely girl like that.
MARGARET:	Is she —
STANDISH:	Could've been, very easily could've been they said, if it wasn't for me 'phoning. If you ask me you know, I'd blame him, his fault entirely. Young girl like that. Absolute layabout, that's all he was.
MARGARET:	(More calmly than she feels.) Please tell me what happened, will you?
STANDISH:	Went over last night, just being friendly like, 'cos she was on her own. But she didn't seem to want to talk. Then this morning no music, usually puts the radio on full blast, curtains drawn, I thought it was funny. Knocked on the door, no reply — then I heard this groaning noise. So I give the door a shove — and there she was lyin' in the middle of the floor, fully dressed, all this brown stuff comin' out of the corner of her mouth. Thought he might have come back and murdered her or somethin'. So I run over the farm house, used their 'phone ... Standish is my name by the way, George Standish ... (He can't understand why she isn't writing anything down: he looks more closely at her, then past her at the white Mini-Minor.) ... You know, for the police or an ambulance or somethin' ... 'ere, you're not from the press. I've seen you 'ere before in that car.
MARGARET:	Yes, I'm a social worker, I've been —

3 29

STANDISH:

Oh, from the Town Hall are you? Mm. (His expression conveys that he doesn't think a lot of interfering busybodies from the Town Hall.) I see.

There is a struggle within him between curiosity to learn more about the occupants of the other caravan, and a desire to present himself in a favourable light. The latter wins. He goes on talking, following MARGARET as she goes into the caravan.)

If you ask me something ought to be done about him. Not as if he couldn't get work if he really wanted, big hulking chap like that. Half a mind to try and reason with him sometimes. But you know his sort . . . knocking her about all the time he was, a real brute to 'er.

MARGARET:

Did he knock her about?

STANDISH:

(Pauses: he is about to be emphatic, but his certainty evaporates and changes into aggressiveness.) Well if 'e didn't, why was she always shouting and screaming like that then?

(MARGARET wants information, but avoids encouraging him to say something not true.)

MARGARET:

(Quietly) Did you ever actually see him hit her yourself?

STANDISH:

(With too obvious caution.) I heard things. (He folds his arms.) That's all I'm going to say.

MARGARET:

(Quietly) Yes I see, thank you. (She turns and goes back towards her car quickly.)

(STANDISH calls after her, feeling he hasn't made the impression he intended.)

STANDISH:	St. Faith's they've taken her to. Tell 'er I was enquirin', I was worried about her, if she wants a visitor I'd be glad to –
	(The starting-up of the car engine drowns his words and confirms in his opinion the general unsatisfactory nature of social workers. STANDISH goes back inside his caravan. MARGARET drives off along the track back across the field.)
	(In a curtained-off cubicle in a general ward of a hospital SHEILA, comatose, is in bed. From outside the curtains are drawn aside by SISTER POTTS, a plump middle-aged woman, who lets MARGARET through. SISTER POTTS disapproves of people who attempt suicide; her behaviour is correct but not sympathetic.)
POTTS:	She'll be all right, they pumped her out, she'll recover.
MARGARET:	May I wait a while?
POTTS:	If you wish, yes. She won't have much to say for herself for a few hours yet though.
	(There is a chair by the bed. MARGAR sits on it, watching SHEILA's pallid and motionless face. She is detached, but puzzled and concerned. She tries to instil some kind of communication between them, but it is too soon yet. Sometimes SHEILA's eyes momentarily flicker open, but she does not know where she is or that MARGARET is there.)

(The interplay of their faces is cut-in
between the flashback scenes which
follow. The first flashbacks are aural,
voices-over against faces. The first is
over SHEILA's face.)

VOICE: Well well well well, and that brings us
                  up to Radio News time . . .

VOICE: (Over MARGARET's face: AUDREY
                  CAMPBELL's voice.) A risk. What
                  you have to ask yourself is whether and
                  why you're prepared to take it . . .

VOICE: (Over SHEILA's face.) Brrrr baby it's
                  cold outside, but here we go then, and
                  this week straight from 17 to number
                  7 . . .

VOICE: (Over MARGARET's face: EDDIE's
                  voice.) A dead loss - a dead loss,
                  ain't I?

                  (Then, over SHEILA's face, the sound
                  of a baby crying and crying; a bright
                  light is shining and hurting her eyes;
                  and the baby is crying and crying.

                  It is the sun which is shining into her
                  eyes as she makes her way round a
                  field along a narrow path by a hedge.
                  This is the first time we see SHEILA
                  properly. A lithe young body, nice legs,
                  a naturally sinuous walk. A striking
                  looking girl at a distance, who neither
                  needs nor wears much make-up to make
                  men turn their heads. A thick-knit open
                  cardigan over a crumpled red shirt-
                  type blouse, with missing buttons; a blue
                  denim skirt, and skimpy sandals.
                  Untidy, she doesn't make the best of
                  herself, having neither the means nor
                  the concern.

                  In her arms she carries a bundle,
                  humped up onto her shoulder: it is her

4 month old baby daughter MANDY, cocooned in a soiled cot blanket and almost invisible. SHEILA carries her like an awkward parcel, never drawing the blanket aside to look at her face. She comes up out onto the road and walks towards a bus stop. There is no bus, and none in sight. She walks on.

The beginnings of a small town, and on the outskirts of it the hospital, so SHEILA doesn't have far to walk. She turns in at the first gate and goes into the main entrance, then after a moment comes out again and goes on across the front of the hospital. Near the railings across the other side of the grass some workmen are digging a hole: one of them wolf whistles. She is used to this and ignores it. At the corner of the building she turns into a yard with space for ambulances. At the side is an entrance marked 'Casualty Department' and she goes in.

Inside, it is busy, with patients sitting on comfortably upholstered benches, and doorways to different clinics round the sides of the room. SHEILA goes to the reception desk.)

RECEPTIONIST: Good morning, can I help you?

SHEILA: There's somethin' the matter with my baby, I —

RECEPTIONIST: Have you been here before? (SHEILA shakes her head.) May I have your name and address then, please?

SHEILA: Gosse, Mrs Sheila Gosse.

RECEPTIONIST: With an 'e' is that, Gosse with an 'e'? (SHEILA nods.) And the baby's name?

SHEILA: Mandy.

RECEPTIONIST: Amanda?

SHEILA: What? No, Mandy. Look, can't you get
                  somebody to —

RECEPTIONIST: Just a few basic details, it won't take a
                  moment. Could I have your address?

SHEILA: Potter's Lane.

RECEPTIONIST: Number? (SHEILA looks blank.) What
                  number Potter's Lane?

SHEILA: No number. Just Potter's Lane. Oh
                  put Potter's Lane Farm, strewth it's
                  taken me three quarters of an hour to
                  walk 'ere, do you 'ave to waste any
                  more —

RECEPTIONIST: I'll put your card straight through now
                  Mrs Gosse, someone will be along in a
                  moment if you'd like to take a seat over
                  there.

                  (Truculently, SHEILA sits on the end of
                  one of the benches. Further along a
                  woman PATIENT smiles, ready to start
                  a chat. SHEILA gives her a stony
                  glance and turns away. She fishes a
                  crumpled cigarette packet out of her
                  pocket and struggles to hitch up the
                  baby so she can light the cigarette.
                  A West Indian NURSE is passing.)

NURSE: No smokin'.

                  (She gestures at the notice which
                  SHEILA would have seen if she hadn't
                  turned away from the PATIENT who
                  wanted to chat. Exasperated, SHEILA
                  picks up a newspaper someone had left
                  on the bench, glances at it, puts it
                  down. Another PATIENT, a man,
                  with his leg in plaster, hobbles past
                  assisted by a NURSE and goes straight
                  into one of the side rooms. This annoys
                  SHEILA. As soon as the NURSE comes
                  back, she rises to her feet.)

SHEILA: Look, can't someone see me, I've been
                 'ere nearly ten minutes, I've got a very
                 sick baby, I want —

                 (Further down the waiting room, the
                 West Indian NURSE is calling out a
                 name with increasing emphasis, trying
                 to find its owner.)

NURSE: Mrs Gosey . . . Mrs Gosey . . .
                 Mrs Gosey!

                 (As the name sinks in, SHEILA turns
                 away from the NURSE she has been
                 speaking to and goes over to the West
                 Indian NURSE.)

                 Mrs Gosey, Potter's Lane Farm?
                 Would you come this way please?

SHEILA: About bloody time.   And it's Gosse.
                 (She goes through the door which the
                 NURSE is holding open, into a small
                 ward with a cubicle in it.)

NURSE: The Sister there'll see to you:
                 Mrs Gosey, Sister.

                 (SISTER THOMPSON is a brisk
                 angular woman of 50, adept at dealing
                 with remarks that she doesn't want to
                 answer by pretending not to have heard
                 them.)

SHEILA: Takes you long enough dunnit, I've been
                 out there with my little girl nearly —

THOMPSON: May I have her then please, thank you,
                 now let's have a look, shall we? (She
                 has the baby out of SHEILA's arms
                 and laid on one of the cubicle beds
                 before SHEILA can even protest.
                 She unwraps the blanket gently but
                 makes no attempt to remove it. She
                 stands over the baby, looks at it for
                 a moment, and then turns to SHEILA.)

135

HOMPSON: Cont)	(Conversationally) What happened to her?
HEILA:	Dunno. She was like that when I come to get 'er up this mornin'.
HOMPSON:	Any vomiting? Has she been sick?
HEILA:	No. 'Ardly took anythin' to eat yesterday, never made a sound all night, I thought she was just sleepin'. Took one look at 'er when I woke up, thought I'd better bring 'er straight 'ere.
HOMPSON:	Yes, you were quite right. (To a passing DOCTOR in an overall.) Doctor Dhondi, would you have a look at this baby please?
	(The passing CASUALTY DOCTOR, a Pakistani, stops to examine the baby. SHEILA tries to see what is going on but SISTER THOMPSON is between her and the DOCTOR and the baby. SISTER THOMPSON and the DOCTOR put their heads together over the baby, murmuring a few words.)
SHEILA:	P'raps she could've swallowed somethin', a pin or a button do you think?
THOMPSON:	(Looking up.) She's not had an accident has she, a fall or a bump on the head or anything like that?
SHEILA:	(Frowning) No . . . no, nothin' like that.
THOMPSON:	Doctor thinks our Consultant Paediatrician should see your little girl. Perhaps if you'd like to take a seat out there in the waiting room until —
SHEILA:	But that's my baby, I want to know what you're —
THOMPSON:	(To the West Indian NURSE.) Nurse, go and find Doctor Cunningham, tell him

THOMPSON: (Cont)	Doctor Dhondi would like him to come at once if he can please. (To Sheila.) You could get some tea in the waiting room Mrs Gosse. I think it would be better if you left her with us, she's quite all right here.
	(SISTER THOMPSON draws the curtain round the cubicle, shutting herself inside. SHEILA hovers uncertainly, trying to catch what is being said, but cannot. She takes out her cigarette packet, then exasperatedly puts it away again. She starts to move reluctantly back to the waiting room.
	Coming towards the cubicle is a brisk young Consultant, JOHN CUNNINGHAM he greets one or two patients he knows, brushes past SHEILA and goes to a curtained-off cubicle. SISTER THOMP puts her head out between the curtains.
	Dr Cunningham, the child's in this cubicle, Dr Dhondi said she shouldn't be moved.
CUNNINGHAM:	Yes, quite right, thank you Sister. (He goes inside the cubicle and SISTER THOMPSON draws the curtains behind him again. There is more murmuring of voices, and SHEILA again tries to hear. After a moment, SISTER THOMPSON comes out and addresses another NURSE.)
THOMPSON:	Nurse, ring through to X-ray, say Dr Cunningham wants them to bring dow their portable machine please. Right away please Nurse. (To SHEILA, pleasantly.) I'm afraid you're going to be in for quite a wait, Mrs Gosse, I'm sure you could do with a cup of tea.
	(SHEILA takes a couple of paces away, stops, turns.)

HEILA:

I've just remembered – she did have a sort of, well, a little tumble the day before yesterday. But that couldn't – it couldn't have been that though, could it?

(SHEILA is sitting in CUNNINGHAM's office, opposite to him across his desk.)

CUNNINGHAM:

Well yes indeed it really could Mrs Gosse. Small babies are very fragile, what to an adult would be a light knock could be much more serious to a baby as young as yours. At the moment she's extremely poorly, that's why I've had to admit her – she needs intensive care for the next few days.

SHEILA:

But what's the matter with her?

CUNNINGHAM:

I can't say definitely until we know the result of the X-ray, but she has the symptoms of a depressed fracture of the skull. She did have a fall, you say?

SHEILA:

Not really a fall, more a sort of a tumble. She seemed all right a few minutes after, I never thought no more about it.

CUNNINGHAM:

How did it happen?

SHEILA:

She was sort of sittin' on the floor like and then she kind of fell over like they do, they do fall over backwards at that age sometimes don't they? She cried, I picked 'er up and – well th - at was all.

CUNNINGHAM:

Did she hit her head on a toy on the floor, the cross-bar of a chair, or something?

SHEILA:

No nothin'. She just kind of flopped back that's all, like that. (A very slight imitating movement with her head by SHEILA. CUNNINGHAM is watching her closely, but is careful to conceal that he is watching her. The telephone rings on his desk.)

CUNNINGHAM:	Yes? (Pause) Where? (Pause: then, non-commitally.) Uh-hum. Right, thank you. (He replaces the receiver. Until now CUNNINGHAM's questions have been information-seeking routine. But from here onwards he knows he's got to be very careful indeed, and above all convey nothing of the suspicion forming in his mind. His voice becomes quiet and casual.) Is your floor carpeted, Mrs Gosse?
SHEILA:	No, lino; we live in a caravan.
CUNNINGHAM:	Very cramped, is it?
SHEILA:	Well, does get a bit cramped, yes.
CUNNINGHAM:	But of course with your husband out all day . . . ? (SHEILA looks puzzled.) He is out at work?
SHEILA:	No, 'e's lookin' for a job. 'E was out though when this 'appened.
CUNNINGHAM:	(Nods) Would you just, erm — just show me again exactly how it happened?
SHEILA:	Well — (Imitating) — sort of like that, that's all.
CUNNINGHAM:	And she's had no other bang or fall of any kind recently?
SHEILA:	No, not that I know of. Is all doctors coloured now?
CUNNINGHAM:	Pardon?
SHEILA:	The doctors — are they all coloured, the ones 'ere I mean, apart from you?
CUNNINGHAM:	I really don't know, I haven't looked recently. Mrs Gosse — (Nodding at the telephone.) — the X-ray confirms a fracture, as I thought. I wonder if you'd come back with your husband this afternoon, would you?

SHEILA: Come back with - well yes, we'll be
                 wanting to come and visit 'er, won't we,
                 yes.

CUNNINGHAM: At about quarter past two?

SHEILA: Yes, all right. (She gets up and goes to
                 the door.) I dunno what he's goin' to say,
                 though. I mean is it very serious, will
                 she be -

CUNNINGHAM: She's in good hands, don't worry we shall
                 take every care of her.

SHEILA: (Nods) It's rotten, isn't it? (She goes
                 out of the door.)

                 (CUNNINGHAM taps his teeth reflect-
                 ively with a pencil, looking after her.
                 Slowly he manoeuvers his swivel chair
                 until he is back up against the wall. He
                 begins gently to bang his head against
                 the wall, trying to re-create the move-
                 ment of falling onto a hard surface. He
                 puts his finger-tips under the curve of
                 his skull, moves his head forward and
                 bangs it back against the wall, trying to
                 trap his fingers. It can't be done. The
                 more he tilts his head back, the deeper
                 the hollow becomes and the more easily
                 his fingers can slide free from the spot
                 where the fracture was. Satisfied, he
                 lunges his chair forward to the desk,
                 picks up the telephone and dials a
                 single-digit number.)

CUNNINGHAM: Is Mr Foster there please? (Pause) Alec,
                 I want a complete skeletal survey done on
                 the Gosse baby admitted about half an
                 hour ago; can you possibly let me have it
                 for two o'clock?

                 (MARGARET is sitting by SHEILA's bed.
                 SHEILA is still unconscious.)

(CUT TO X-ray plates on an illuminated
screen in CUNNINGHAM's office. Just
finishing a conversation about them are
CUNNINGHAM and the hospital radiolog;
MR FOSTER, a middle-aged man.
CUNNINGHAM crosses to his desk and
picks up the 'phone.)

CUNNINGHAM: Ask them to come in Miss Hamilton
please - and bring your notebook, will
you, I want a record of every word that',
said. (He replaces the 'phone and starts
to arrange what chairs there are in his
office, placing two of them opposite him
at his desk.) If they'd been any later, I'd
have had to have handed the whole thing
over to Dr Fazarki. They'd have loved
that.

(A tap on the door, and MISS HAMILTON
ushers in SHEILA, followed by EDDIE
GOSSE and SISTER THOMPSON.
MISS HAMILTON is young, wears specta
and is ordinary looking — which certainly
could not be said of EDDIE GOSSE. He i,
gigantic man, in his early forties, going
bald, as powerfully built as a gorilla; thi
black eyebrows, a battered face, and an
open-necked shirt displaying a hairy ches
But despite this appearance and a gritty
growl of a voice, EDDIE's nature is in fa
gentle and kind. He is amiable, garrulou
and naive; there is nothing ingratiating
about his friendliness toward everyone, a
he has long since ceased noticing the effe
his appearance has on people. When he i,
nervous, as he is now, he compensates w:
ebullience. CUNNINGHAM glances at his
watch.)

I was beginning to wonder if you were —

EDDIE: (Jumping straight in.) Yes well blame me
for that Doctor, not 'er, I was 'avin' a kip
yer see, she tried ter get me up, then I

EDDIE:(Cont)   cut meself shavin', my fault in the first place 'avin' ter 'urry yer see . . .

CUNNINGHAM: My name is Cunningham, I'm the Consultant Paedia —

(EDDIE shakes him warmly by the hand.)

EDDIE: Very pleased ter meet yer, Doctor; Gosse, Eddie Gosse, 'ow do you do?

CUNNINGHAM: This is Mr Foster, our Radiologist, and —

EDDIE: (Pumping Mr Foster's hand up and down.) 'Ow are yer Mr Foster, all right?

CUNNINGHAM: (Mumbling) Miss Hamilton is my secretary —

(As EDDIE moves rapidly in her direction, MISS HAMILTON jumps up, dropping her notebook and pencil, which EDDIE scoops up with one hand while he shakes her hand with the other.)

EDDIE: Miss 'amilton, nice ter meet yer, sorry that was my fault, yer needn't 'ave got up.

CUNNINGHAM: (Desperately interrupting.) Perhaps if you'd sit down, Mr and Mrs Gosse?

EDDIE: Yeh ta — whoops! (This because the chair seems rather unsafe under his weight.)

CUNNINGHAM: I've asked these people to be present because —

EDDIE: (A quick look round.) Sort of conference is it? Yes; well then I'd like to kick off by sayin' something straight out.

CUNNINGHAM: (Not expecting this.) Oh. Yes?

EDDIE: Yes. (An announcement.) Every confidence! I just wanted to say that, that's all. Perfectly satisfied, me and my wife, aren't we love? You'll pull our Mandy through,

EDDIE:(Cont)	we believe that, we're sure of it.
CUNNINGHAM:	Mr Gosse, I think I should make it clear
EDDIE:	(Going on.) Nobody's goin' to 'ear a word out of me against 'ospitals and nurses, I can tell you, I think they're the most —
SHEILA:	(Hissing) Eddie!
EDDIE:	Eh? Oh sorry, manners, shouldn't interrupt, no. (He notices MISS HAMILTON struggling to keep up her shorthand notes) 'Ello, what's she doin' then?
CUNNINGHAM:	Miss Hamilton is here at my request to take a note of this conversation, Mr Gosse.
EDDIE:	(Amiably) Oh Gawd, and me rabbitin' on and on. Sorry Miss, I won't say another word; right Doctor, carry on.
CUNNINGHAM:	As your wife will have told you, I'm the Consultant Paediatrician here. (EDDIE opens his mouth.) That is, I specialise in small children and babies. (EDDIE nods. Mr Foster is the head of the Radiology Department.
EDDIE:	(Smiling) I know what those are, that's X-rays innit, yeh. (Pleased with himself he looks at SHEILA for approval; and gets only a black look in return.)
CUNNINGHAM:	Your daughter's head was X-rayed this morning. Alec?
	(FOSTER switches on the light on the X-ray screen, and CUNNINGHAM moves over to point out something on the plate.)
	This shows, as I told you Mrs Gosse, that she has a depressed fracture here. (He indicates it on the back of his own head.)
EDDIE:	That's serious innit?
CUNNINGHAM:	It could not have been caused in any other

CUNNINGHAM: Cont)	way than by a blow at that exact point. You described to me how she fell over backwards and hit her head, Mrs Gosse.
EDDIE:	'S amazin', you'd never believe it could 'appen.
CUNNINGHAM:	(Quietly) No you would not. Because you see the fall you described Mrs Gosse — I asked you to tell me about it twice, and show me exactly how she fell — that fall in my opinion could not have caused a fracture in that place. (Pause) I was wondering if there was any other suggestion either of you could make as to how it might have happened. (Another pause.) Please think carefully before you say anything.
	(SHEILA's face is mask-like and expressionless: EDDIE is frowning hard with the effort of thinking.)
EDDIE:	I am thinkin'. I dunno what to say though, 's a mystery. (To SHEILA.) She couldn't've fallen down the steps, could she, no 'course she couldn't, you'd've remembered. Anyway, never left 'er on 'er own, did yer, no yer wouldn't do that would yer. (To CUNNINGHAM.) Must've been a real 'ard bang though mustn't it, it is, it's a real mystery.
CUNNINGHAM:	I should make one thing absolutely clear. Anything said in this office is entirely confidential. Miss Hamilton's notes, I give you my word, are only for my own records.
EDDIE:	Yeh well I mean you take that for granted don't yer, with doctors and that, 'course, yeh. Honest, I don't know what to say, do you love?
CUNNINGHAM:	(Casually) Do you hit her sometimes when she's naughty, Mr Gosse?

EDDIE:	(Not offended.) No, I don't 'old with 'ittin' kids, neither of us do.
CUNNINGHAM:	I'm sorry if this causes you offence Mr Gosse, but I must put this question directly to your wife. Have you ever see your husband hit your child?
SHEILA:	(Shaking her head several times.) No. N I don't think so.
EDDIE:	(Reproving her gently.) Give 'im a straig answer to a straight question love. Neve mind you don't think so — just 'ave you, 'aven't you?
SHEILA:	No I haven't.
CUNNINGHAM:	Have you hit her yourself ever, in a fit o temper or —
EDDIE:	'It 'er own kid? Look at 'er, she wouldn' 'urt a fly, would yer?
CUNNINGHAM:	Mr Foster?

(This is too serious now for him to be anything but formal. FOSTER takes off the plates of the X-rays of the baby's skull, and replaces it on the screen with two others. He pulls the screen forward so that CUNNINGHAM can point on it from his desk.)

I must ask you to look carefully at these please. As well as X-raying your baby's head, at my request Mr Foster also did a skeletal survey — that is, he X-rayed her entire body and limbs. This picture is of your child's upper left forearm about here. (He points on his own arm.) It clearly shows a healed fracture there, of a break which occurred four or five weeks ago. The other picture is of the right ribs: there are two healed fractures, one there and the other just above it. They were probably both caused at the same time; they're about seven or eight weeks old.

EDDIE: (Rising, his mouth opening and shutting, as he goes over towards the X-ray screen.) Let me look! Show me! I – ah yes but – I mean, 'oo can tell from that 'oo it is, I mean it might be anybody's baby for all we know, 'oo's to say –

FOSTER: (Firmly) I am, Mr Gosse. These are X-ray pictures of your baby.

EDDIE: (Near incoherance.) Jesus Christ I – Sheila – Sheila, do you know what they're saying, that's our Mandy!

CUNNINGHAM: To a powerfully built man, Mr Gosse, what might seem like a slight tap –

EDDIE: (Horrified) No – no – never – I've never 'it 'er, never. (He slumps in his chair.)

THOMPSON: It's clearly obvious that the child has been hit and –

(CUNNINGHAM silences her with a gesture. He then repeats words he hopes he has correctly memorised, but from time to time he has to glance down at a paper on his desk to make sure that he gets them right.)

CUNNINGHAM: Mr and Mrs Gosse, it is my duty to tell you that I am not satisfied by what you have said. I believe this child's injuries are not capable of having been caused by any known form of illness or disease, and that therefore there are grounds for suspecting that they must have been inflicted on her by some person or persons in her home environment. And it is also my duty to inform the appropriate authorities that that is my opinion.

(Total silence. SHEILA's face is blank; EDDIE's is a conflict of emotions, until the implications of CUNNINGHAM's last words sink in.)

EDDIE: What do yer mean, the authorities, wha authorities? You mean the police? (He rises from his chair, taking SHEILA's arm.) Come on Sheila, we're not stoppir 'ere listenin' to any more of this —

CUNNINGHAM: Just a moment. (EDDIE stops and turns. It could be the police Mr Gosse, but it doesn't have to be. Whether it is or not depends on you. But if you leave now I'n afraid I shall have no alternative.

EDDIE: What's that supposed to mean exactly, th

CUNNINGHAM: I can't guarantee the police won't at som later stage be brought into it, but I'm prepared to leave the decision with some one else if you co-operate with them.

EDDIE: (Suspiciously) Someone else like 'oo?

CUNNINGHAM: I'd ask someone from the Local Children Department or the NSPCC to call at your home and make a report.

SHEILA: (To EDDIE.) I'm not 'avin' no-one from the Children's Department comin' round!

EDDIE: And I'm not 'avin' the cruelty people eith

CUNNINGHAM: Then that leaves me with no alternative.

EDDIE: I — I — oh all right then, the Children's Department.

SHEILA: (Straight at him.) If they come, I go. I mean that Eddie.

EDDIE: What, you'd sooner 'ave the cruelty man in 'is uniform with everyone —

CUNNINGHAM: They don't wear uniforms nowadays Mr Gosse.

EDDIE: (To Sheila.) Why not the Children's Department? Why not? (SHEILA doesn't answer; she just looks away.) I don't believe it, I can't, honest I . . . (He puts his arm round her shoulder to take her ou and turns.) It doesn't mean we can't — w

EDDIE:(Cont)	can still come and see 'er though, can't we?
CUNNINGHAM:	Yes of course. You'll be at home later this afternoon?
EDDIE:	(Taken aback.) This after — well, yeh, we'll 'ave to be, won't we? (Looking round.) Honest I . . . (Defeated) All right, love, come on. (He takes SHEILA by the arm and they go out.)
	(When they have gone, a silence falls. CUNNINGHAM's face shows the strain he has been under during the interview. SISTER THOMPSON is thin-lipped.)
THOMPSON:	If I may say so, Sir, in my opinion you should inform the police — it's obvious by his behaviour he's already got a record and —
CUNNINGHAM:	(Strained, snapping.) Nobody asked for your opinion! (Calming) I'm sorry Sister. You may well be right. However . . . Miss Hamilton, get me the NSPCC will you please?
	(In the hospital ward cubicle, MARGARET is still sitting at SHEILA's bedside.)
	(The white Mini-Minor stops in front of a farm. A woman points the way through to the field where the caravans are. The car drives on. SHEILA is sitting on the caravan steps smoking; playing on the ground nearby is TIMMY, a small boy of 4. He is cleanly and neatly dressed. MARGARET gets out of the car, and goes over to SHEILA.)
MARGARET:	Mrs Gosse? Good afternoon, my name's Margaret Ashdown. I'm from the NSPCC.

SHEILA: (Shouting) Eddie. Eddie! (EDDIE comes
out from behind one of the canvas screen
round the toilet.) It's the cruelty people

(MARGARET stands, looking at TIMMY.
EDDIE comes over, a surprised look on
his face. He towers over MARGARET.
She smiles at him pleasantly.)

EDDIE: What, you from the — strewth! Well,
er — Timmy, say good afternoon to this
lady, she's — erm well, come on, say
good afternoon then.

MARGARET: (To TIMMY.) Hello, who are you then?

(TIMMY goes to EDDIE, who picks him
up in his arms.)

EDDIE: This is our —

TIMMY: Number one!

EDDIE: Number one, that's it, that's right! Well
look, you'd best play out here a bit, me
and your Mum's got to have a talk with
this lady for a few minutes, see. Don't
go out of sight now will you, there's a
good lad. (To SHEILA.) Well open the
door for 'er, love.

(SHEILA has remained unmoving on the
steps. With bad grace she gets up and
opens the door. MARGARET has to squee
past her to get inside. EDDIE follows
MARGARET, but SHEILA remains outsid

Within, the caravan is untidy and poorly
furnished. It has a two-tiered bunk at
one end, with a curtain. At the other en
EDDIE and SHEILA's bed folds up during
the day into a window seat. A laminate-to
table folds out from one wall: against the
other is a small sink and a small calor-
gas stove.)

EDDIE: (Cont)	'Ere, I think we'll 'ave you out for a start.
	(He picks up a large black mongrel dog which is asleep on the day-bed, and pushes it out of the door, addressing SHEILA outside as he does so.)
	Well come on in love, I expect the lady'll want to talk to both of us. (To MARGARET.) My name's Eddie Gosse. (For once he does not ebulliently shake her hand, but simply stands nervously looking at her.)
MARGARET:	I'm Margaret Ashdown. May I sit here? (She sits on the day-bed, at ease.)
	(Grumpily, SHEILA comes in. EDDIE starts to tidy up things from the table.)
EDDIE:	I'm afraid it's a bit untidy, I – would yer like a cup of tea?
MARGARET:	Thank you yes, I'd love one.
EDDIE:	(Feeling the tea-pot.) 'Ot it up a bit, love, will yer?
MARGARET:	Do you mind if I smoke? (EDDIE shakes his head.) Mrs Gosse?
SHEILA:	(Sourly) No thanks. (To rub the point home, soon afterwards she lights one of her own cigarettes.)
EDDIE:	(To MARGARET.) Bit short of room as you can see. (He clears his throat.) So – well – it's you 'oo's got to decide, is it? I mean, like, what's goin' to 'appen then?
MARGARET:	Not on my own. I'll talk it over with my supervisor Miss Campbell and with Dr Cunningham.
SHEILA:	(Flat) You're from the Children's Department.

(MARGARET opens her handbag and take
out an identification card. She passes it
to EDDIE who without looking at it hands
it on to SHEILA. SHEILA glances at it,
then hands it back to EDDIE and turns
away.)

EDDIE: (To SHEILA.) Why should she say she
was if she wasn't?

(SHEILA ignores him.)

MARGARET: I'm afraid I'll have to start by asking you
one or two questions –

EDDIE: 'Course, well, that's why you come,
innit, yeh.

(MARGARET is determined to progress
calmly and in a low key. She takes out a
small notebook, in which she will make
brief notes and expand them later from
memory.)

MARGARET: Mr E Gosse and Mrs S Gosse, is that
right? And just the two children, Timmy
and Mandy isn't it? How old is Timmy?

EDDIE: Four. (To SHEILA.) Four last month
wan'e?

MARGARET: And you rent this caravan from Mr Sykes
at the farm? How long have you been
here?

EDDIE: Three weeks - three weeks tomorrow.

MARGARET: Where were you living before?

EDDIE: Birming'am. 'Ad a job up there but I got
the sack. 'Eard there was work goin'
round 'ere so - well 'ere we are.

MARGARET: Where are you working now, what sort
of work do you do?

SHEILA:	'E starts Monday.
EDDIE:	(Gently reproving her.) Look, love, what's the point? (To MARGARET.) I'm not workin', I 'aven't got a job.
MARGARET:	You're signed on at the Labour Exchange?
EDDIE:	Well I - no. 'Ad a bit of back pay yer see, when they stood me off up there.
MARGARET:	What kind of work do you do, Mr Gosse?
EDDIE:	Oh, you know - anythin', Farm work, labourin', buildin' sites, bit of buyin' and sellin' junk, anythin' that comes.
MARGARET:	You've found nothing round here yet though?
EDDIE:	(Shaking his head.) I'll say the next bit for you, shall I? I've not really looked all that 'ard, yeh, I know.
MARGARET:	How long have you been married?
SHEILA:	Five years.
EDDIE:	(Flatly, correcting her.) Six months. (Nodding in the direction of outside.) 'E's not mine, Timmy, 'e's 'ers by another feller she knew before me.
MARGARET:	Does he pay maintenance to you for him, Mrs Gosse? (SHEILA snorts.) I'd like to see Timmy again before I go. Is he outside?
EDDIE:	Yeh, you get 'im love, will yer?
SHEILA:	(Going to the door and shouting.) Timmy! Come in 'ere a minute, this lady wants to talk to yer. Come on, 'urry up.
	(It is the dog who is first in through the door, followed by TIMMY.)
EDDIE:	Eh, not you, 'oppit, go on, gerrout! (He pushes the dog out, then sniffs.)

EDDIE: (Cont)   Timmy, Gawd, where've yer been,
stand still. (He bends down and looks at
the child's feet.) 'Ow many times 'ave
I told you to watch where you're walkin'
in that field, eh? Come on, let's 'ave
these off, that's it, that's the way.
(To MARGARET.) Sorry Miss. Pooh,
there's only one place for these. (He
opens the caravan door and throws the
shoes out; then immediately realises his
mistake.) Strewth, now what've I –
Sherbert, leave 'em, Sherbert!

SHEILA: Oh you stupid – I'll get 'em. (She picks
up the radio she has brought in with
her and takes it out again, shouting.)
Sherbert! Come back 'ere! Sherbert!

EDDIE: (To TIMMY.) 'Ang on a minute now,
let's find yer slippers. Right, come on,
give us yer foot that's it, now the other
one, there we are. Now then, this lady
wants to talk to you, all right? (He
picks the child up and sits with him on
his knee: TIMMY shyly hides his face
against his neck.) Come on, sit up,
there's a good lad, she's not goin' to
bite yer. (To MARGARET.) Sorry,
'e's always a bit shy with strangers at
first: I'll 'ave to stay till 'e's got used
to yer, 'e'll be all right then with yer
on 'is own.

(This huge man's gentleness and the
overwhelmingly obvious affection of the
child for him, and him for the child,
leaves MARGARET nonplussed.)

Speak up nice and clear for the lady now,
will yer? She's goin' to ask yer a few
questions, so you tell 'er whatever she
wants to know, all right?

MARGARET: I don't think I need to bother him today,
I just wanted to see him, that's all.

DDIE: (Brushing the child's hair out of his eyes with his hand.) Fine lookin' young chap, innee? Got yer Mum's eyes, 'aven't yer, eh? (Awkwardly as a thought strikes him.) Did yer want - I mean - would yer like 'im to take 'is shirt off or anythin'?

MARGARET: No that won't be necessary. Thank you for coming in to see me Timmy, you go off and play again if you want to.

(TIMMY whispers something in EDDIE's ear.)

EDDIE: Oh all right, you monkey, come on then. Up we go! (He swings Timmy up so that he can reach an open tin on top of a cupboard. TIMMY takes out some sweets.) 'Ere, I thought yer said one, not two; oh go on, take another one for yer Mum then. Right, off yer go - and eh, watch where you're walkin' now, we don't want them slippers covered in cow muck too. (TIMMY goes out.) She always keeps 'im clean yer know, it's not just today. 'E's a good little kid. (He sits.)

MARGARET: Mr Gosse, I can't hope to get a proper picture on one visit like this, obviously I shall need to drop in quite a lot.

EDDIE: Yeh, 'course you will. Anytime yer like, there's always one of us 'ere. I - well I don't always get up every mornin', I might not - if you don't mind me sort of not bein' properly dressed and that, I —

MARGARET: Oh don't bother about that, that won't matter.

EDDIE: (Sadly) She does 'er best to keep things tidy, but it's not easy with two kids, an' me layin' around ... anyway, if yer say yer don't mind ... (pause) All right then, yes, well, what next?

MARGARET:	Were you expecting me to ask you something else?
EDDIE:	They usually do.
MARGARET:	'They'?
EDDIE:	'Oo ever it is, you know - welfare, assistance, WVS, Council - we've 'ad them all. 'Ad a clergyman once, I think it was Derby, no it was Preston.
MARGARET:	You've moved around a lot?
EDDIE:	Dozens of places, must be 'undreds by now. Always been like that: thought I might change with Sheila but . . .
MARGARET:	(A thought suddenly striking her.) Your rent's paid here, is it?
EDDIE:	One week: We 'ad to put it down in advance. Old man Sykes 's already mentioned it a couple of times. Yer can't really expect 'im ter go on waitin' for ever though, can yer?
MARGARET:	The Social Security people, the Assistanc Board, they'd help with the rent.
EDDIE:	That mean's signin' on though, dunnit? All those questions, why don't you do this where's your cards, 'oo was your last employer . . . I get . . . it makes me feel . . . (He is beginning to perspire, and wipes his forehead.) I just can't stand answerin' people's questions, yer see.
MARGARET:	You've answered all mine.
EDDIE:	(It had not struck him.) Yeh - yeh I 'ave, 'aven't I? Funny, that.
MARGARET:	May I ask you just one more? What exactly do you live on?

ƆDIE:	Like I said, bit of work, sellin' stuff, old bedsteads, anythin' people leave lyin' around outside their 'ouses. They'll even give you a few bob for takin' it away sometimes. (He goes to the window of the caravan and looks out.) She'll 'ave 'ad enough one day, you couldn't blame 'er. Could get 'erself a decent feller if she wanted to, couldn't she?
ꟾARGARET:	But she hasn't.
ƊDIE:	Even waited for me ...
ꟾARGARET:	'Waited'? (EDDIE nods.) When was that?
ꞈDDIE:	When I was in the nick. Two lots of six months I've done: only one since I've been with 'er though. The other one was oh, seven, eight years back now.
ꟾARGARET:	Would you tell me what for?
ꞈDDIE:	The first, what was it - copper tubin' I think. Knew it was nicked, should never 'ave touched it, this feller offered it me cheap, desperate to get rid of it, I suppose. Law come round, there it all was, lyin' in the 'allway, couldn't miss it. (Embarrassed.) She doesn't know about that though, it was before I met 'er, yer see, I've - if you wouldn't mind not mentionin' it ...
ꟾARGARET:	No of course. And the other?
EDDIE:	Yes, she knew about that. Breakin' and enterin' - or tryin' to. Kicked in a shop door, what do they call it, a lingerie shop. Saw this nightie in the window, it was 'er birthday comin' up. Ten o'clock at night, dark; stupid, I never think yer know ... middle of the 'Igh Street, the copper was down on me before I'd even got the door open ... (He shakes his head at the futility of it.) I never thought

EDDIE: (Cont)	she'd wait, but she did.
MARGARET:	(Quietly) Just those two convictions? (EDDIE nods: MARGARET gets up.) Well - thank you for telling me, I'll come again in the morning, Mr Gosse.
EDDIE:	(Rising, towering above her.) Yeh, right. Funny, innit? Don't seem to mind you. You don't start layin' down the law like most of 'em.
MARGARET:	(Smiling) I still might though.
EDDIE:	(Seriously) There's one - I mean, I've answered your questions, would you answer one for me? You don't, not seriously, you don't think I'd 'alf kill me own kid, do you?
MARGARET:	I don't know, Mr Gosse: I honestly can't say.
EDDIE:	Yeh - well, that's straight.

(He opens the caravan door and stands back to let MARGARET go out first. On the grass outside SHEILA is lying with her transistor radio, and smoking. TIMMY is playing near-by. MARGARET goes to her car, saying 'Good bye Mrs Gosse' and 'Good bye Timmy' as she goes. As she gets to the car, SHEILA turns up the volume of the radio, very loud.)

(In the office of her supervisor, AUDREY CAMPBELL, MARGARET is edgy: one of AUDREY's concerns is to try and maintain detachment.)

MARGARET:	There's another child there. I've left it, and I don't know if I ought to have done.
AUDREY:	A risk. What you have to ask yourself is whether and why you're prepared to take it.

MARGARET:	If I'm going to establish a relationship I've got to get a footing. To remove the other child immediately would put both their backs up. Hers is up already, but his at least doesn't appear to be.
AUDREY:	How do you mean, 'appear'?
MARGARET:	Is he pretending to me, putting on an act? I don't think he's capable of it; he's a very nervous, insecure sort of man, I don't think he could carry off a bluff. He's not clever, even as a criminal: petty, stupid things he's done, that's all.
AUDREY:	He says.
MARGARET:	Honestly Audrey though, I'm inclined to believe him. No work pattern, no spontaneous aggression, even towards the dog. It was quite genuine that he loves the little boy. More importantly, the little boy obviously loves him, clings to him for protection and shelter. I don't think he'd do that if he had any fear of him.
AUDREY:	The 'one child' theory? (MARGARET looks at her questioningly.) That it's sometimes only the one child, the one that's considered to be 'unsatisfactory'. I had a case myself a few years back, five children in the family, four of them treated normally, only the one who was slightly backward got knocked about, because he was a disappointment. But of course occasionally if you remove the battered one, they turn on one of the others.
MARGARET:	Yes, but Timmy's over four. That's a bit old for this kind of battering isn't it? (A nod from AUDREY.) Anyway, if we took the child, they could and probably would both pack up and disappear. They live in a caravan, they're quite accustomed to moving on the spur of the moment -

MARGARET: (Cont)	especially when the rent's overdue, which I gather it already is. No, I'm going to take the risk, leave the child there for tonight. Somehow I just don't think anything'll happen. I only hope I' not making a terrible mistake.
	(In the hospital cubicle: MARGARET's face, and SHEILA's face.)
	(The next morning MARGARET is knocking on the door of the caravan. There is no reply. She walks round to the side; the curtains are drawn. She goes up the steps and knocks once more After a delay EDDIE opens the door, singlet and trousers just pulled on, rubbing his face with his hands to try an wake himself up.)
EDDIE:	(Astonished at the earliness of her arrival.) Cor bloody 'ell!
MARGARET:	I hope you don't mind me coming so earl I've a long round to do today, it just happened I'm passing this way first.
EDDIE:	What time is it then?
MARGARET:	Quarter past nine.
EDDIE:	Can you give us a minute or two?
MARGARET:	Yes of course.
EDDIE:	(Reaching behind him for the dog and bundling it out.) Go on then, out yer go. Sheila. Sheila! Miss Whatsit's 'ere.
	(MARGARET goes back to wait by the ca One by one the caravan window curtains are pulled back. EDDIE re-appears at the door with his shirt on. He nods across t MARGARET and she goes to the caravan.

Inside, a touselled SHEILA in a flowered
nylon dressing gown is putting on the
kettle and yawning. Their bed is still
pulled down: at the other end the bunk
bed is concealed by a curtain pulled
across it.)

MARGARET: I'm sorry to come so early; this was the
most convenient way I could work it in.

SHEILA: (Half awake, washing out cups at the sink.)
Where's me bloody fags gone Eddie?

EDDIE: Where'd you leave them? There they are
look, on the floor.

SHEILA: I ought to be gettin' off to the 'ospital.
(To MARGARET.) You've no news 'ave
yer? How she is?

MARGARET: I rang the hospital, they said she's about
the same. (Casually) How's Timmy this
morning?

EDDIE: (Nodding towards the bunk.) Still fast
asleep by the sound of it.

SHEILA: That was your fault lettin' 'im stop up so
late, wannit?

EDDIE: Kids! They never want to go to bed do
they?

MARGARET: May I just have a peep at him?

(She is not waiting for the answer and is
moving down to the end of the caravan as
she says it. She pulls back the curtain
and looks, then very slowly turns. The
bunks are both empty. EDDIE is unable
to think of anything better to say than the
obvious.)

EDDIE: 'E's not there. 'E'll 'ave gone out early,
playin', 'e often slips out before we -

MARGARET: (Quietly) I'd like to see him please
Mr Gosse.

EDDIE: Yeh ... (He goes to the caravan door ar
           calls.) Timmy! Timmy! (He turns bac
           and sits.) The number of times I've tol
           'im not to go out without lettin' us know.

SHEILA: Tellin' 'im, what's the good of that, 'e'l
           never learn that way. Anythin' could 'a
           'appened, 'e could've wandered off and
           got lost, fallen in the stream, anythin' -
           and 'ow would we know?

EDDIE: I was the same when I was a kid - if the
           sun was shinin' I was off and out as soon
           as I woke up.

MARGARET: (Firmly) I would like to see him please,
           Mr Gosse.

EDDIE: Yeh ... well I dunno, don't even know
           where to start lookin'. You wouldn't be
           passin' this way again later would you?

MARGARET: No, I'm not.

SHEILA: Oh 'ave a cup of tea first, then we'd best
           go out an' -

MARGARET: (Firmly) Let's go and look for him now,
           shall we?

           (Provocatively, SHEILA puts a mug of te.
           in front of EDDIE. EDDIE looks at her,
           then looks at the implaccable MARGARET

EDDIE: I'll get me shoes.

           (He puts his shoes on, and goes out of the
           caravan, followed by MARGARET.
           SHEILA picks up his mug and empties the
           tea down the sink in annoyance.)

           (Outside EDDIE and MARGARET go round
           the back of the farmyard, with EDDIE
           shouting the child's name.)

EDDIE: (Suddenly) Eh! An' what do you think
           you're up to then? Didn't you 'ear me

EDDIE: (Cont)   shoutin'? (TIMMY is playing behind one of the buildings. EDDIE goes to him, picks him up, puts him down again.) Yer Mum's makin' yer breakfast. Aren't you 'ungry? Go on then, off you go. (TIMMY trots back towards the caravan.) I'll 'ave ter put a bolt or somethin' on that door. She's right yer know, anythin' could 'appen to 'im.

MARGARET: I'm sorry I had to be so insistent.

EDDIE: 'S all right. (Pause) I - could we - could we talk a few minutes before we go back?

MARGARET: Yes of course.

(They sit on a low farm cart which is at the end of the yard.)

EDDIE: (Not looking at MARGARET while he speaks.) I get a bit lost when it comes ter talkin'. Don't talk a lot - 'cept when I'm nervous: then I don't say anythin'. I was wonderin' if you could 'elp. Yer see - it's me.

(MARGARET looks at him, startled: but he does not notice.)

A dead loss ain' I? Other people can work, do a job, can't they? Me, I ... look, even just talkin' about it. (He wipes at the perspiration which is forming on his face with his fingers.) I don't know what's the matter, they look at me, they say a great big chap like that ... but all I wanna do is lay around an' sleep, I'm - I feel tired all the time. Doin' nothin' - and I'm tired. (He looks at her.) Well at least you don't try and talk me out of it like most of 'em do.

MARGARET: I don't really know you very well yet.

EDDIE: They usually start straight in 'cos I'm l
          'Cos they're scared of me I suppose,
          scared of the size of me.

MARGARET: (Quietly) Of your physical strength?

EDDIE: (Quiet laugh.) Like the way yer put tha
          yeh. Used to 'ave a job boxin' in a boot
          on a fair ground. Young lads used ter
          think they was terrific, Jack the Giant
          Killers. Anyone could knock me over,
          balance, no fight, no guts. Can't think,
          can't work, can't even ... (Looking ove
          towards the caravan.) We're both too
          tired now. (He shakes his head.) She
          won't stop long.

MARGARET: Has she said so?

EDDIE: No, no she 'asn't - except yesterday
          mornin', that was the first time; when
          they said up at the 'ospital they'd call th
          Children's Department people in.

MARGARET: Why does she feel so strongly about ther
          (EDDIE shakes his head, puzzled.) Did
          you ask her about it afterwards?

EDDIE: Yeh. Just said she didn't want to talk
          about it. Funny kid, can't tell what she'
          thinking at all sometimes.

MARGARET: She's good with the children?

EDDIE: Devoted to Timmy. Can't 'ave 'ad an
          easy time, not married, feller left 'er,
          didn't want to know.

MARGARET: When you first met her, did you mind
          Timmy or would you sooner she'd -

EDDIE: Oh no, no question of that, the kid was
          everythin' to 'er. I mean 'e's a lovely
          kid innee, never entered me 'ead, no-one
          part with someone like 'im.

MARGARET: Have you been married yourself before?

EDDIE: (A quick turn of his head towards her, an

EDDIE: (Cont)   a slight smile.) You don't miss much, do you? Twelve years ago, two kids, one'll be ten or eleven now, the other one I suppose about eight. She got married... 'aven't seen or 'eard anythin' of them for years.

MARGARET: Why were you divorced, would you mind telling me?

EDDIE: 'E 'ad a decent job, set 'er up in a 'ouse of their own, everythin'. Yer couldn't blame 'er, could yer, me just the same then as I am now. She went to live with 'im, the divorce was straightforward, that was the end of that. I thought that was the end of me too; never thought I'd meet someone like Sheila. Might've been different if we'd met when I was younger - she might even've got me workin'.

MARGARET: But she can't now?

EDDIE: (Shakes his head.) Too old to change... beautiful girl... two kids... I think every day it can't go on, it won't last.

MARGARET: So you do the one thing that makes sure it won't?

EDDIE: Yeh, that's true, innit, when you put it like that? But why? (He gets up.) Well, you've got a lot of calls to do, 'aven't you? Thanks anyway. (He stretches out his hand to help her down from where she is sitting on the cart.)

MARGARET: I'll come again tomorrow - but not quite so early.

     (As they approach the caravan, pandemonium breaks out inside it. TIMMY is yelling, the dog is barking, and SHEILA is shouting. EDDIE and MARGARET run over to it, and EDDIE opens the door. Inside, SHEILA is in a fury.)

SHEILA:	For Gawd's sake get that bloody dog out of 'ere, get 'im out! Bloody mongrel, o all the stupid things to 'ave in a place like this!

(TIMMY has a slight cut over one eye which is bleeding. EDDIE picks him up to comfort him, and at the same time pushes the dog out. He finds a cloth and wipes TIMMY's face with it, making a stream of soothing remarks.)

SHEILA:	It was your idea to 'ave 'im, but you're not the one that's got to try and live with 'im under your feet all day, oh no. You' out wanderin' about, God knows where you -

EDDIE:	All right love, all right, calm down. (To TIMMY.) Come on son, it's not bad, see it's stopped bleedin' already. There's a brave chap, tell yer what, let's find then sweets shall we? Come on then, up yer go! (He lifts TIMMY up to the sweet tin, and down again.) All right? All right no are you? (TIMMY nods.) What 'appened then?

SHEILA:	That bloody animal, knocked 'im flyin', fell right against that thing there, could'v taken 'is eye out.

(EDDIE looks at TIMMY: MARGARET looks at SHEILA.)

EDDIE:	Well, never mind, it didn't, 'e's OK. Sorry about that, Miss.

MARGARET:	Don't apologise, it wasn't your fault; I'm glad it's nothing serious.

SHEILA:	(Yelling) It bloody is serious!

MARGARET:	(After a pause.) Yes. Well - I'll come again tomorrow.

(MARGARET goes out. SHEILA is crashing out, still in a fury.)

SHEILA: Why didn't you come back with 'im, yer knew I was doin' 'is breakfast, I can't tidy up and do everythin' and keep my eye on 'im and watch the dog an' -

EDDIE: Sorry love. We was 'avin' a bit of a chat.

SHEILA: Oh yes, I could see that from the window. What about?

EDDIE: Nothin' special, just this and that. She's nice, easy to talk to, I like 'er.

SHEILA: So I've noticed. What the 'ell does she 'ave to come snoopin' round first thing in the mornin' for?

EDDIE: Yer mean - yer mean yer didn't know? Don't be silly love -

SHEILA: Well 'ow should I? You're the one she does all the talkin' to.

EDDIE: Well you talk to 'er next time, I'll keep out. She's different from the others, you'll -

SHEILA: She's no different at all, she's like all the rest of 'em - only prettier.

EDDIE: Now don't be silly love, she's -

SHEILA: Don't keep sayin' 'Don't be silly', can't yer think of nothin' else? P'raps you think I'm silly 'cos she's clever and posh spoken, is that it? Fancy a clever bird do yer?

EDDIE: (To TIMMY.) Feelin' all right now son are yer? Wanna go out again? 'Ere - take yer milk with yer. Only don't go out of the field now, OK? (TIMMY nods, and goes out.)

SHEILA: Tellin' 'im, tellin' 'im - that's all you ever do. 'E doesn't take a bloody scrap of notice.

EDDIE:	'Ell, 'e's only four, innee?
SHEILA:	Nobody kept their 'ands off me 'cos I wa: four.
EDDIE:	Oh all right. 'Ere, where's me tea?
SHEILA:	Thrown it away, didn't think you'd be wantin' it, sooner be sittin' out in the field with that little piece. I could see yer, yer know.
EDDIE:	Then yer could see yer didn't 'ave nothin to worry about, couldn't yer?
SHEILA:	(Mockingly imitating.) Oh please 'elp me up, you big strong man, I'm too little to get off this cart on me own.
EDDIE:	Eh? (He goes over to her and puts his arms round her.) She's not my type now, is she?
SHEILA:	I dunno, she seems keen enough on comin round ter see yer.
EDDIE:	Well I've just told yer, next time you talk to 'er.
SHEILA:	No thanks. But just let 'er try anythin' o: with you an' I'll -
EDDIE:	(Still with his arms round her.) Oh don't be si - look, tell you what, we could go back to bed for a bit if yer like.
SHEILA:	No thanks. (Suddenly she kisses him, the puts her face against his chest.)
EDDIE:	(Calmingly) I'll make yer a nice cup of te then, eh? (Pause) What was 'e doin'?
SHEILA:	Standin' there talkin' to me.
EDDIE:	No, I mean the dog.
SHEILA:	'E was jumpin' up tryin ter get a piece of bread off the side there.
EDDIE:	(Thoughtfully) Yeh you were right, it wasn't a good idea 'avin' 'im. But I didn't know 'e'd grow so big. (Pause) Well we'd

DDIE: (Cont)	best get off down the 'ospital. Dunno if we ought to take Timmy, I think he might be a bit frightened. Do yer think the man in the next van'd keep an eye on 'im an hour or two?
HEILA:	I dunno what 'e's like. Only seen 'im a couple of times comin' across the field.
DDIE:	Go and ask 'im, will yer?
HEILA:	Why me?
DDIE:	(Grins) Well no-one can say no to you, can they?
HEILA:	Oh, all right. (She opens the caravan door; as she does so, the dog is heard barking outside.)
DDIE:	I'll 'ave to do somethin' about that dog, love.
	(Outside, SHEILA is over at the next caravan, and knocking at the door. STANDISH opens it.)
HEILA:	Good mornin', I'm from the next -
STANDISH:	Caravan. Wonderin' 'ow long it'd be before you'd pop over. Anytime, don't 'esitate, only too ready to be of assistance.
HEILA:	I've got to go to the 'ospital to see my baby, I was wonderin' if you could -
STANDISH:	Oh sorry to 'ear that, nothin' serious?
HEILA:	I dunno. I was wondering if I could ask you - we've got another little boy yer see and we didn't really want to take 'im with us -
STANDISH:	Seen 'im. Nice little lad. Got 'is Mum's eyes, 'asn't 'e? Don't give it another thought, I'll be 'ere all the time, I'll see 'e comes to no 'arm.
SHEILA:	Thanks. Oh, 'is name's -

STANDISH: Timmy. 'Eard you callin' 'im. Now an
             time, you know, if yer just feel like
             poppin' over for a chat or anythin', don'
             'ave ter 'ave an excuse, not with neigh-
             bours, do yer?

SHEILA: Yeh, well, we'll be gettin' off then.
             Thanks very much.

             (STANDISH's eyes follow her as she ma]
             her way back to her own caravan.)

             (In the hospital ward SHEILA is still
             unconscious. MARGARET is looking at
             her. She remembers the crying of
             TIMMY and the barking of the dog.)

             (MARGARET has pulled up her car by th
             roadside in a lane and is dictating notes
             her visit into a battery-operated miniatu
             tape recorder.)

MARGARET: Something about the incident of the child
             being hurt by the dog. It appears to be
             genuine, and yet there was a quality in th
             woman's anger almost as though it was
             being deliberately generated...

             (Her voice carries on, and it is now com:
             out of the tape recorder as it lies in fron'
             of her on the desk in AUDREY CAMPBEL
             office.)

             ... I made a mistake in stopping talking :
             long to him. He wanted to talk, but it mu
             have looked bad in her eyes. (She presse
             the button and stops the tape recorder.)

AUDREY: It wasn't very good to let that situation
             arise, was it? What were you doing -
             proving to yourself you weren't afraid of
             him?

MARGARET:	(Wryly) Yes, probably, I think so.
AUDREY:	Well that's understandable.
MARGARET:	It's ironic - nothing happened in the night when I was scared it might, then the child was injured when I was actually there; my presence might even have caused it.
AUDREY:	It could have been an accident. It's a very explosive situation, isn't it? Our main responsibility is the safety of the child, but we mustn't show it to them. We've got to try and handle it in a way that won't make them feel they're under attack, because that could easily trigger off another battering...
MARGARET:	I feel I ought to postpone one of my other calls and go back there. You see if she did hit that child this morning, then she's probably been hitting the baby as well. I don't think he's got any idea, and I don't know how he'll react if he finds out. Up till now he's been able to avoid thinking about it, but now he's got to - and I don't know what he'll do when he does.
	(EDDIE is walking aimlessly round the stalls of a market. He has the dog on a lead, and keeps tugging it along. At a pet stall he enquires if the PROPRIETOR would buy it. The PROPRIETOR shakes his head.
	EDDIE goes on. As he comes out of the market he passes a PDSA van. A MAN is coming down the steps at the back of it, wearing a white over-all. He sees EDDIE with the dog.)
MAN:	Can I help you?

(EDDIE shakes his head, and walks
quickly on. Eventually he comes out on
a patch of waste ground, and sits. He
picks up a piece of tubing aimlessly, the
puts it down. After a few moments two
other dogs playing on the other side of the
waste ground catch his eye. He looks
down at his own dog; then slowly he
unfastens its collar and gives it a slight
push. It runs off over to the other dogs
and begins to play with them. When the
camera returns to where EDDIE was
sitting, we see he is no longer there.)

(MARGARET is at the door of the Gosse'
caravan. From the steps she can see
TIMMY playing round the back of it. She
waves to him, and he waves back. After
keeping her waiting, SHEILA eventually
opens the door.)

MARGARET: Hello Mrs Gosse. How are you?

(SHEILA makes no reply, simply leaves
the door open and goes back to the sink
where she is washing up. On the draining
board at the side the radio is on, loud.
MARGARET has to try and make herself
heard over it.)

How was Mandy today?

SHEILA: Par'on? (Reluctantly she turns off the
radio.)

MARGARET: I said how was Mandy today?

SHEILA: Dunno. We 'aven't been. Eddie was
supposed to be comin' back to take me.
'E's been out since this mornin'.
(Unkindly) I thought 'e might 'ave been
comin' to see you. You don't 'ave any
fags on yer, do yer? Eddie was goin' to
bring me some.

¡ARGARET:	(Offering her packet of cigarettes.) While there's an opportunity Mrs Gosse I'd like to talk to you about the rent. Mr Sykes might be persuaded not to press for it for a week or two. But we shall have to take some steps to get it paid. I mentioned it to your husband, if he signed on -
HEILA:	You're wastin' your time.
¡ARGARET:	Couldn't you persuade him?
¡HEILA:	No.
¡ARGARET:	I would like to be able to help but -
¡HEILA:	We don't want any 'elp.
¡ARGARET:	Well even the first point, the question of having Mandy back again -
¡HEILA:	Question, what question? She's our kid, no-one can stop us -
MARGARET:	They can: and they very well might.
SHEILA:	(Outraged) Our own kid, stop 'er comin' back to -
MARGARET:	Mrs Gosse - surely you can see at this stage she can't be allowed back here?
SHEILA:	Well of all the bloody - just because she had an accident with -
MARGARET:	It wasn't one accident - it was three. And until we understand exactly how she got those injuries, there's no question of letting her come back. I'm empowered to apply to a magistrate for her to be kept temporarily in a place of safety.
SHEILA:	I knew it, I bloody knew it. You're from the Children's Department.
MARGARET:	(Quietly) No I'm not.
SHEILA:	Well why do you talk exactly like them then?
	(A pause: because in her anger she has

172

given herself away, and knows it. Tight
lipped, she turns her back on
MARGARET and goes on with the
washing-up.)

MARGARET: You've had dealings with them before?
(No response.) It would save a lot of
time if you'd tell me. (No response.)
Think it over Mrs Gosse, will you?

(EDDIE comes in through the caravan
door, followed by TIMMY. Not seeing
TIMMY, SHEILA flies off the handle, on
restraining herself at EDDIE's reprovin
glance and nod in the child's direction.)

SHEILA: You bloody idle bastard, where the 'ell d
you think -

EDDIE: Sorry love, I - I got 'eld up. (He takes
off his jacket and puts it over a chair.)
Afternoon, Miss. (He picks up TIMMY
gently and sits him on the edge of the
table.) Look son, I've got some bad new
I've got to tell yer. I took Sherbert out
with me, and well, I've lost 'im. (He
takes the lead out of his trouser pocket.)
'Is lead broke, yer see, 'e run off. Spent
hours lookin' for 'im but... (So far
TIMMY hasn't reacted at all, apart from
looking up at him wide-eyed.) Look, tell
you what, 'ow about if we went down the
market next week an' bought yer another
one, a nice new little puppy, would that b
all right? Eh? (TIMMY nods and smiles
Good lad, right then, that's what we'll do
'Ere, let's find you a couple of sweets
shall we? (He gets the tin down and
presses a handful of sweets into TIMMY's
hand. TIMMY smiles and runs off with
them out of the caravan.) Well I'm...
aren't kids funny? 'Ere's me been tryin'
ter pluck up courage all the way 'ome ter
tell 'im.

MARGARET: He seems to have taken it well enough.
Well I was just on my way, Mr Gosse,
so I'll say good-bye.

EDDIE: Oh, well, yeh, if yer must. Sheila
looked after yer all right, did she, give
yer a cup of tea an' that?

MARGARET: We had a little chat and so on, she'll tell
you about it. I'll drop in tomorrow
sometime I expect, just for a few
minutes. Good-bye; good-bye Mrs Gosse.

(MARGARET goes out, and can be heard
calling 'good-bye' to TIMMY outside the
caravan.)

SHEILA: Where the 'ell 'ave you been, I've been
waitin' hours.

EDDIE: (Sitting) I couldn't know I was gonna lose
the dog could I? Put the kettle on love, I
could do with a cup of tea. Any'ow, you
'ad a bit of a chance for a chat with 'er;
get on all right did yer?

SHEILA: We didn't talk about anythin' - just the
weather an' that. Did yer bring me them
fags?

EDDIE: Yeh, in the jacket. (He takes off his shoes.)

(SHEILA has her back to him and is feeling
in the jacket pocket for the cigarettes. She
finds something else.)

SHEILA: (Casually) 'Ow did yer say yer lost 'im
then?

EDDIE: Like I said, 'is lead come off - and 'e was
away.

SHEILA: (Turning, with the dog's collar in her hand.)
With you chasing along beside 'im, unfast-
enin' 'is collar while 'e was runnin', I
suppose?

EDDIE: (After an embarrassed pause.) Well... no

EDDIE: (Cont)   yer see what really 'appened... Oh
                Sheila, I 'ad to, din I? I tried ter sell
                'im, then I thought of 'avin' 'im put down
                but... I couldn't think what to do, I 'ad t
                get rid of 'im.

                (SHEILA throws down the collar in
                disgust, goes to the sink to wash up som
                more cups, and flips on the radio.
                EDDIE gets up and goes over, and
                switches it off.)

EDDIE: Sheila - I 'ad to. You know I 'ad to.

SHEILA: Why did you? Why did you 'ave to?

EDDIE: (Desperately) You know why! All those
                people, everyone at the 'ospital, even
                Miss what's 'er name! They think I did i
                to Mandy, Sheila! An' don't yer see - al
                the time it was that bloody great dog!
                Look what 'e did to Timmy yesterday -
                an' if 'e'd really 'urt 'im bad, I'd've
                been... Jesus, Sheila, you know what 'e
                did to our Mandy, 'e nearly killed 'er.
                When she come back we'd never 'ave a
                moment's -

SHEILA: (Flat) She's not comin' back.

EDDIE: What? You don't mean she's - you 'aven't
                'eard from the 'ospital that she's -

SHEILA: (Still flat.) No, she's all right. It's your
                fancy little piece 'oo says she can't come
                back 'ere, not even when she's better.

EDDIE: Well yer see then! I was right! They did,
                they all thought it was me; but now the
                dog's gone, that solves it. It was the righ
                thing to do, there yer are, I knew it was.

                (EDDIE has moved away down the
                caravan to the table. SHEILA stops
                moving the cups around in the washing-up
                basin. There is a pause.)

SHEILA: (Quiet) It wasn't the dog.

EDDIE: (Angrily) It was!

SHEILA: It wasn't the dog!

               (At the other end of the caravan, EDDIE
               turns very slowly and looks towards her.)

               (In the hospital ward, SHEILA's lips are
               moving, but her voice is very faint.)

SHEILA: Eddie?

MARGARET: Mrs Gosse? It's all right, you're in
               hospital.

               (SHEILA licks her lips, swallows
               uncomfortably, turns her head and looks
               at MARGARET beseechingly: she wants a
               drink of water. MARGARET helps her to
               take a sip from the cup at the side of the
               bed.

               SHEILA lies back. She begins very
               quietly to cry. MARGARET says nothing,
               simply sits and waits. She puts her hand
               on SHEILA's which lies by her side on the
               bed.)

MARGARET: Is there anything you'd like me to do?
               (No response.) Would you like me to
               come and see you tomorrow?

               (SHEILA, crying silently, shakes her
               head. MARGARET turns to go. It is only
               as she reaches the curtains at the end of
               the cubicle that SHEILA speaks.)

SHEILA: Please, yes...

               (What follows would of necessity transpire
               over a very long period of time. It is

clear that the subsequent conversations
occur at intervals during this period.)

(A few days later MARGARET comes to
see SHEILA in hospital. The cubicle
curtains are now drawn back so that her
bed is open to the rest of the ward. Whe:
MARGARET comes, SHEILA is lying
down and is very tired. She sees
MARGARET standing by the side of the
bed.)

SHEILA: My baby...

MARGARET: I've just been up to have a look at her,
                 she's making good progress.

SHEILA: No, Timmy...

MARGARET: We've no news, I'm afraid. How are you
                 feeling?

SHEILA: He... you don't know where he...?

MARGARET: I'm afraid not, not yet. We're still
                 trying to find them.

SHEILA: 'E's taken 'im away... you'll never find
                 'im... never...

(On another day, MARGARET is talking t∙
SISTER POTTS at the end of SHEILA's be∙
They think SHEILA is asleep.)

SISTER POTTS: There's been no sign of the husband. Do
                 you think he'll come??

MARGARET: I don't know.

SISTER POTTS: It's her baby Sister Wain's got up on her
                 ward, isn't it? (MARGARET nods.)
                 Some people get away with a lot don't they
                 If there's one thing I can't stand it's -

                 (They notice that SHEILA is awake.
                 SISTER POTTS goes off down the ward.

MARGARET comes to the side of
SHEILA's bed.)

SHEILA: (In a low voice.) Do they all know what I
done?

MARGARET: No, only two or three of them.

SHEILA: They send women like me to prison don't
they?

MARGARET: (Quietly) No, not always.

SHEILA: 'E nearly got done for it, and I was goin'
to let everyone think that -

MARGARET: But you didn't. (Pause) Why did you
eventually tell him?

SHEILA: I 'ad to... the dog, I didn't know what
would 'appen next, I... I'd never 'it
Timmy before, never, I was scared, I
thought I was goin' to start on 'im... they
should 'ave left me, why did they 'ave
to... He hates me. His face, it... 'e
just looked, that's all... didn't speak or
anythin' when I told 'im, 'e just looked.
'E sat there lookin' and lookin', then he
got up and started to pack up 'is things
and Timmy's... 'E didn't say a single word,
just packed up and went. At the finish I was
'ittin' 'im, tryin' to stop 'im... but 'e went,
'e went, 'e went...

(MARGARET is in AUDREY CAMPBELL's
office.)

MARGARET: And so that was that. And then, I don't
know when, sometime in the night or the
early hours of the morning, she took the
whatever it was and tried to kill herself.

AUDREY: He didn't hit her, that must have been very
- it must have been a far more painful
experience than any amount of physical
violence: she was used to it, she'd expect

AUDREY: (Cont)   that. She took it for granted that was what you did to people, it had been done to her always I suppose... However, th immediate practical details, we'll have to think of those. Where's she going to stay when she comes out of hospital?

MARGARET: She can't be left on her own, she might

AUDREY: Would she go into a hostel or something like that?

MARGARET: She wouldn't stay long if she did, she'd almost certainly have a row with the people in charge and walk out. It needs to be somewhere where she can be on he own and yet _not_ be on her own, where there's somebody around all the time... wonder? Mrs Sykes seemed a nice sympathetic sort of woman when I talked to her, I wonder if she'd...

(SHEILA is in a room on the first floor o the farm house. MARGARET is there, helping to give it some kind of character and homeliness. SHEILA is standing looking at her, with her back to the window.)

SHEILA: And she really said I could stay 'ere for . bit?

MARGARET: For a while, until we can make other arrangements. She says they don't use this room since her daughter's married. Oh, and I'm making the necessary arrangements to get your Social Security Benefit.

SHEILA: Does she know?

MARGARET: No, only that your baby's had some kind of accident, that's all.

SHEILA: Are you goin' to tell 'er? (MARGARET shakes her head.) But she'll want to know

SHEILA: (Cont)	where Eddie is, why he's gone away, why I tried to -
MARGARET:	She knows husbands leave their wives, and that wives sometimes get depressed - I don't think she'll ask a lot of questions.
SHEILA:	But you, she knows about you.
MARGARET:	That I'm a social worker with families, that's all.
SHEILA:	Are you going to take me to court?
MARGARET:	Sheila, I - look, perhaps we could have a talk and get a few points cleared up could we, if you feel like it? Wouldn't you like to sit down?

(MARGARET sits on the edge of the bed:
SHEILA remains standing and lights a
cigarette. Nevertheless after a time she
does move away from the window and go
to sit at the table.)

MARGARET:	You ask me if we're going to prosecute you. The answer is no. I don't think to punish you would achieve anything. You punish yourself anyway, I think you always have. Were you punished a lot when you were a child?
SHEILA:	Only when I done wrong.
MARGARET:	What was 'wrong'?
SHEILA:	(She tries to explain: she tries to speak and can't; her shoulders suddenly sag.) Everythin'.
MARGARET:	Who to, your mother and father, just one of them, or -
SHEILA:	I didn't 'ave a father, not one that I remember any'ow. Only a lot of... uncles. She used to tell me if it 'adn't been for me she could've got someone nice to marry 'er, 'ad a good 'ome and...

SHEILA: (Cont)   (A clear recollection of what her mother used to say.) 'Oo'd take me with a dirty messy kid like you? (She stabs her cigarette out ferociously.) Christ, I 'ated that bloody woman, I 'ated 'er, I 'ated men, I 'ated... (Flatly) everybody. I ran away when I was fourteen, I met that Scotch bastard ponce, 'e wanted me to...

(They are sitting in a not very prepossessing cafe, at a corner table, having a cup of tea.)

SHEILA: ... and when I 'ad a kid they said it needed care and protection. I wasn't suitable to look after it, they said. They took it away... fuckin' Children's Department. My own kid - and now I don't know where she is, I 'aven't seen 'er for... 'ave 'er adopted they said, it's the only fair thing for 'er, give 'er a chance. (Suddenly) No, no that's not true, it was me - I told 'em I wanted 'er adopted, I knew Mac, 'e wouldn't 'ave any more to do with me if I - and 'e didn't anyway.

MARGARET: How old were you then?

SHEILA: (Flat) A 'undred...

(They are sitting in MARGARET's car. Outside, the rain is pouring down. The car is stationary, and SHEILA is staring straight ahead out of the windscreen.)

SHEILA: ... nearly seventeen I met this other feller. As soon as I was pregnant 'e didn't want to know. I thought, they're not 'avin' this one, by Christ they're not! I'm goin' to 'ave somethin' that's mine, no-one's goin' to take this one away from

SHEILA: (Cont)   me. That was Timmy. 'E's always been mine, I wouldn't ever let anyone...
(Suddenly and horrifyingly recollecting.)
And then I - 'ow could I do that, 'ow could I - not to Timmy, 'ow could I? That was the first time in 'is life I ever so much as lifted a... What am I? (She turns and looks at MARGARET.) What am I? I remember now... that's what Eddie said. Just as 'e was goin' 'e turned round an' that's what 'e said. 'What <u>are</u> you? An' what's the answer to that?

MARGARET: What would <u>his</u> answer be?

SHEILA: 'S obvious innit? 'E went.

MARGARET: (Quietly) You don't think he'd any idea before, that you'd -

SHEILA: No.

MARGARET: (Quietly) Yes, I think he had. (SHEILA turns to look at her.) He must have had some idea... but he just didn't want to face it.

SHEILA: You mean - 'e knew? But then why did 'e -

MARGARET: Because he loved you.

SHEILA: (Turning away and staring out of the windscreen.) It's only a word, though, innit? 'Love'... 'E's gone.

(MARGARET, again, is in AUDREY CAMPBELL's office.)

AUDREY: It sounds as though you're making some progress at least. You've a long job ahead of you, two years, probably more like three. She's missed an awful lot of mothering, hasn't she? But at least she's beginning to trust you, or it sounds like it. She's starting to talk a bit. It's the same old story isn't it? Her mother bashed her

AUDREY: (Cont)   about, she bashes Mandy, when Mandy grows up she'll probably do the same to her children - unless we can do something to break up the pattern. What abou[t] juvenile court proceedings, by the way, for care and protection? Have you mad[e] up your mind?

MARGARET: No. A lot will depend on how she reacts to me putting Mandy with a foster parent after she's discharged from hospital. If Sheila will accept that, then I'd like to h[er] off. Well, she's waiting next door to se[e] me, I'd better go.

AUDREY: Margaret, why not suggest you go togeth[er] to see her with the foster mother?

(MARGARET nods, and goes out of the door into the next room. SHEILA is sitt[ing] waiting, with an impassive expression. The conversation picks up sometime afte[r] MARGARET has come into this room.)

MARGARET: ... we know Mrs Jackson very well, she['s] a very nice woman. (No response from SHEILA.) It would only be a temporary measure, you mustn't forget that. (No response.) And of course you'd have access, you could go and visit her. (No response.) Sheila I know this isn't going to be easy for you. (No response.) It'd help me if you'd tell me what you feel.

SHEILA: Nothin'. I don't feel nothin'. Why should I?

MARGARET: Because you think I've taken Mandy away from you - isn't that right? (No response[.]) Your first baby the Children's Departmen[t] took away, your second Eddie took away; and now your third I've taken away from you.

SHEILA: (Flatly) That's right.

MARGARET: It isn't right, Sheila. With Mandy the
              situation's different: you <u>can</u> get her
              back, and you will - eventually, if things
              work out. I haven't taken her away
              permanently, and I'm not stopping you
              from seeing her. But I am protecting
              her. I have to. You know that, Sheila -
              and perhaps I have to protect you?
              (Pause)

              (Very slowly SHEILA folds her arms and
              puts them down on the edge of a desk.
              Just as slowly she lowers her head onto
              them.)

              (MARGARET is dictating into her tape
              recorder, in her office.)

MARGARET: That must have hurt. But even then she
              didn't cry; perhaps she won't any more.
              Sometimes reality's too painful for crying
              about.

              (MARGARET and SHEILA are seen coming
              out of a small suburban semi-detached
              house. MARGARET's voice is heard over,
              dictating.)

MARGARET: The baby was discharged from hospital and
              I think she took it quite well when she'd
              seen the foster home we'd arranged for
              her.

              (MARGARET goes to the farm to visit
              SHEILA. SHEILA isn't there; MARGARET
              scribbles a note and leaves it on the table.
              MARGARET's voice is heard over,
              dictating.)

MARGARET: She wasn't at the farm the next time I
              called - she'd gone out shopping. A

MARGARET:
(Cont)

rejection, because I'd put her baby into someone else's care? I shan't really feel happy until I can get her to come with me to Mrs Jackson's regularly to see the baby.

(MARGARET and SHEILA are coming ou of the house where the baby is fostered, and walking down the street together. They are talking quite amiably. MARGARET's voice is heard over, dictating.)

MARGARET:

Well, she's taking it better than I could have hoped. She appears to have accepte for the time being this is the only realistic solution. The house isn't very far from the farm so she can visit fairly regularly. Today she asked if I'd go witl her again the next time.

(MARGARET and AUDREY are in AUDREY's office.)

AUDREY:

And what did you say?

MARGARET:

I said yes of course.

AUDREY:

You'll encourage the dependency for a while?

MARGARET:

She's got to depend on someone, otherwis she'll never learn to cope with this child depending on her.

AUDREY:

She's going to make great demands on you What if she wants to go in an evening or o a Sunday afternoon? (MARGARET shrugs What about your own life?

MARGARET:

My sister's moved in with me now. Well you know her, Audrey. She's got enough social life for both of us.

AUDREY:

Boy friends?

MARGARET: Half a dozen, she's glad when I'm out,
and then she can... it's funny really,
she's been to bed with far more men than
Sheila and yet by middle class standards,
different way of looking at things, she's
considered to be an ordinary nice
respectable girl - because she can look
after herself.

AUDREY: No, I meant you.

MARGARET: I've got no ties at the moment, which is
probably just as well.

AUDREY: You say that as though celibacy was some
kind of social work qualification.

(AUDREY has her hands lightly clasped
on her desk, her left hand uppermost,
and it is ringless. MARGARET looks,
AUDREY knows she is looking: her hand
remains motionless: perfectly lightly
clasped.)

MARGARET: Well, isn't it? At least that's the image.

AUDREY: (Mildly reminiscently.) It used to be...
(Smiles) It is a problem.

MARGARET: (Changing the subject.) I think the next
problem's going to be how Sheila copes
with visiting. I mean, once she starts
doing it on her own without me - whether
she sticks to regular days arranged in
advance, or starts dropping in too often
without any prior warning at all, or
perhaps even begins tailing off, going in
the other direction and gradually abandon-
ing the child.

AUDREY: Yes, I think those are some of the problems,
some of the immediate obvious ones that
might occur during the passage of time.
Doubtless you'll take them one by one as
they crop up - if they crop up - and all the
others too that you haven't thought of, nor

AUDREY: (Cont)   either of us have yet. Well, it's getting
late. I'm going to the theatre tonight.
(She rises and starts putting things in he
bag.)

MARGARET: Have a good time.

(It is late at night. MARGARET and
SHEILA are in the kitchen of the farm
house, MARGARET helping SHEILA with
the washing-up.)

SHEILA: I'd've lived with Eddie without marryin'
'im, it was 'is idea, not mine. Soon as
'e found I was pregnant, nothin' else'd do
it 'ad to be marriage.

MARGARET: Where would he go with a little boy? You
know him - where do you think? (SHEILA
shakes her head.) Try and think.

SHEILA: I wouldn't want you to go after 'im.

MARGARET: Loving you as he does, loving both the
children - he must be terribly lonely and
unhappy. It's something he'll have to
think out for himself, but at least it migh
help if there was someone he could talk to

SHEILA: 'E once worked on a fair ground for a bit
you know, the sort that go round with
circuses. 'E said that was the only job 'e
ever really liked, travellin' round all the
time. Never in one place for more than a
few days. But there must be 'undreds of
'em, you'd never find 'im.

MARGARET: With our organisation, our contacts all
over the country - we might, there is a
chance. You love Timmy very much don'
you?

SHEILA: More than anyone - till I met Eddie. Tha
was the thing about 'im yer see, 'e took
me and the kid straight off. I would've
put the kid away like I done with the other

SHEILA: (Cont)   one if 'e'd asked, but 'e never did. That
was why when we 'ad Mandy - 'avin' a
daughter with Eddie, I thought it was
goin' to be like startin' again...

MARGARET: And Eddie loves Mandy too doesn't he?

SHEILA: Oh yeh, yeh, 'e does. 'E was always on
at me to look after 'er better than I did.
Suppose 'e'll get 'er as well now won't 'e?
I... I am, I'm frightened. It's right yer
see, it's true, I'm not really fit ter 'ave
kids am I?

MARGARET: What was Mandy like when she was born?

SHEILA: 'Orrible. Not like a proper kid at all.
Cryin', wouldn't sleep, wouldn't smile,
wouldn't eat. Never seemed to like me...
dirty, pissin' all over the bed, not like a
proper baby, know what I mean, not like
Timmy... 'e was smashin'. And I thought
Eddie's, he must, 'e was bound to get fed
up with Mandy bein' like that. An' we was
so tired, I never 'ad no time for Eddie or
for anythin'. I wanted it to be a boy for
Eddie, I wished it'd been a boy, 'e
must've wanted one of 'is own, mustn't 'e,
I mean it's only natural for a man. An'
sometimes when she went on cryin' an'
cryin' I could've killed 'er, honest I - (The
great cavern has opened, and SHEILA has
said it and realised she meant exactly
what she said. The cup she is holding in
her hand drops, and smashes on the floor.
She sways, grips the edge of the sink,
stares down at the washing-up water.)
Please... please try and find my Eddie, I
can't go on without my... (SHEILA lifts
her head and looks up out of the window.
Beyond it is a cold and blustery night, and
the wind is savaging at the trees, making
their branches creak and sway.)

(Over them the end titles come up:-)

WHEN THE BOUGH BREAKS

FINISH

68
909K

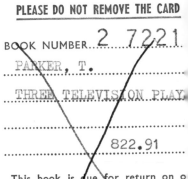